THE MOON IN HAND

THE MOON IN HAND

A Mystical Passage

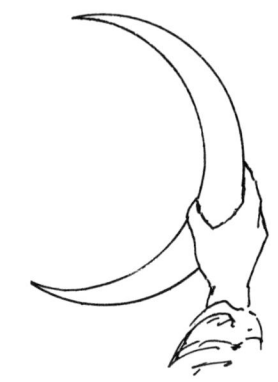

Eclipse

Portland   Maine

Astarte Shell Press
P.O. Box 10453
Portland, Maine 04104

Copyright 1991 by Eclipse
All rights reserved

No part of this book may be used or reproduced in any manner whatsoever without written permission except in the case of brief quotations embodied in critical articles and reviews.

Grateful acknowledgement is made to the following for permission to reprint excerpts from previously published material:

Harper & Row Publishers, San Francisco, CA: "By the Earth that is Her Body" from *The Spiral Dance*, 10th Anniversary Edition, 1989, by Starhawk; and for "The Charge of the Goddess," from *The Spiral Dance*, 1979, by Starhawk.

Z. Budapest for *We All Come From the Goddess*

Sparky T. Rabbit for the *Hecate Chant*

Library of Congress Number 90-085390

ISBN 0-9624626-1-6

Cover design by Eclipse
Book design by Sylvia Sims, Portland, Maine
Illustrations by Eclipse
Typesetting by Briarwynde, Portland, Maine
Printed in the USA by McNaughton & Gunn, Saline, Michigan

1st Printing 1991

10 9 8 7 6 5 4 3 2 1

Dedication

This book is dedicated to our Earth and her children;
To Starhawk, whose beauty moves me;
To Margot Adler, whom I adore and adore;
To Elena Riverstone, who has deeply touched my heart;
And especially to Shaw, who calls me "Mom,"
reminding me to plant my feet firmly on the ground.

Blessed Be.

ACKNOWLEDGEMENTS, THANKS AND INSPIRATIONS

There are many people I wish to thank for their support and skills. This book has taken time, and many friends have pitched in with typing, editing and encouragement. Thank you for all your work from the beginning of this project to now.

I send freedom to my animals for teaching me their ways and for their constant love and distraction. I send my spirit love to Isis, my wolf dog, who with my dear lost Halo, is in spirit. I send love to you, my most wonderful animal companion, Moon-wheat, my blue-eyed dog, who smiles at me every day and makes me happy. Blessed be all puppies for their boundless spirits.

I thank you with gentleness, Elena, for your spirit's whispers and your inner child's love. I love you. I dedicate the stories to you.

I invoke empowerment to all the women who have shown courage in ritual, teaching me the way. Thank you, many times over.

I offer the best to Rowe Conference Center for being intricately connected to my healing.

I share visions with the women of Astarte Shell Press and thank them for believing in this book. Special thanks go to Sapphire for her quiet smiles and support and to Elly with her keen eye for editing and her powerful ability to guide me into words and passages of thought.

Books are not written alone, and my son Shaw has been there, taking charge, keeping an eye on the home and all our pets as I typed year after year. I wish happiness to you, and I thank you for being who you are, my wise one.

I honor the Ancients, who continue to guide me between the worlds. And I acknowledge my trust in the gray-eyed crone who visits me in dreams.

I send abundant joy to Luisah Teish, whose powerful being carries the voice of the Ancients.

I honor Merlin Stone, a very special woman, whose wisdom gives me hope.

And last of all, I return to the beginning, to my childhood, to the fairy tale *At the Back of the North Wind*. I thank North Wind, the woman with long, dark hair, who came in the night and taught children about the door to the Goddess' heart. It is the door I went through to find the land of the Mysteries.

THE WEST

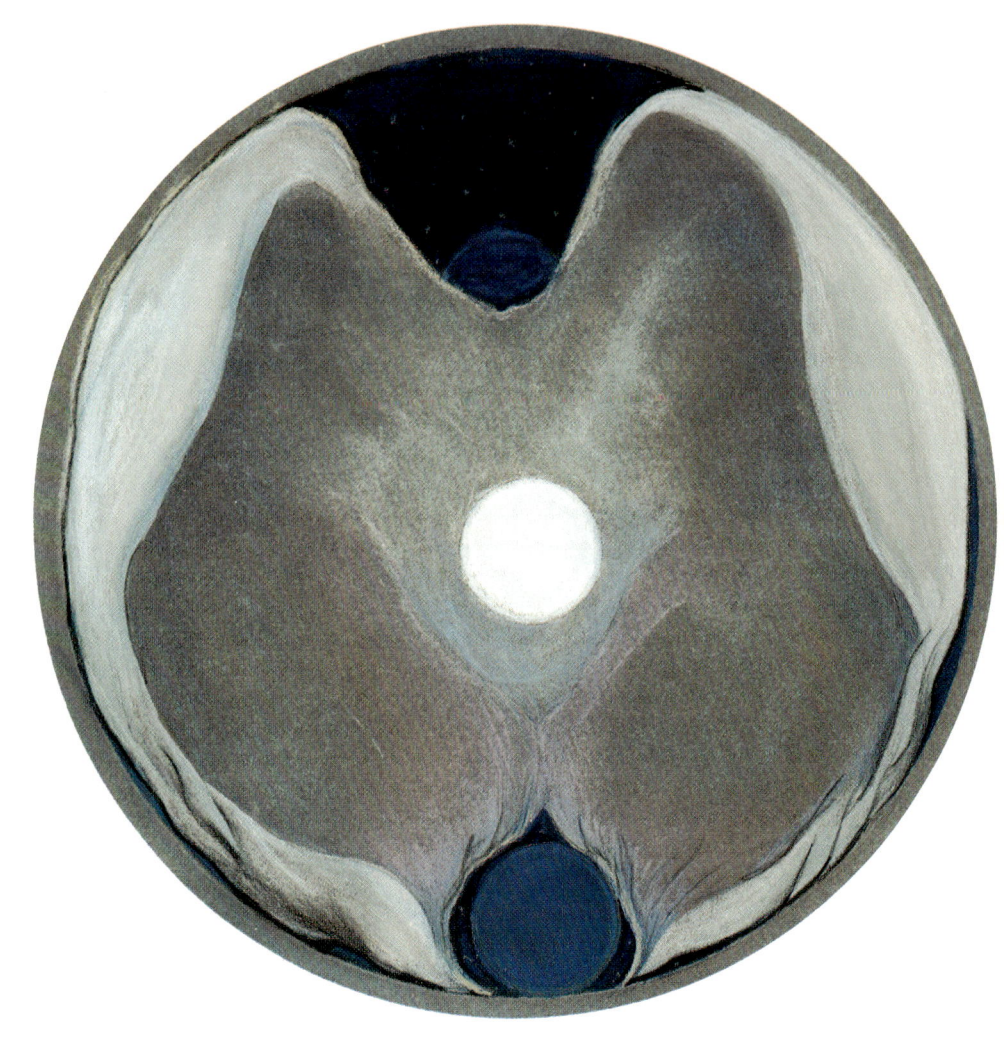

THE NORTH

THE EAST

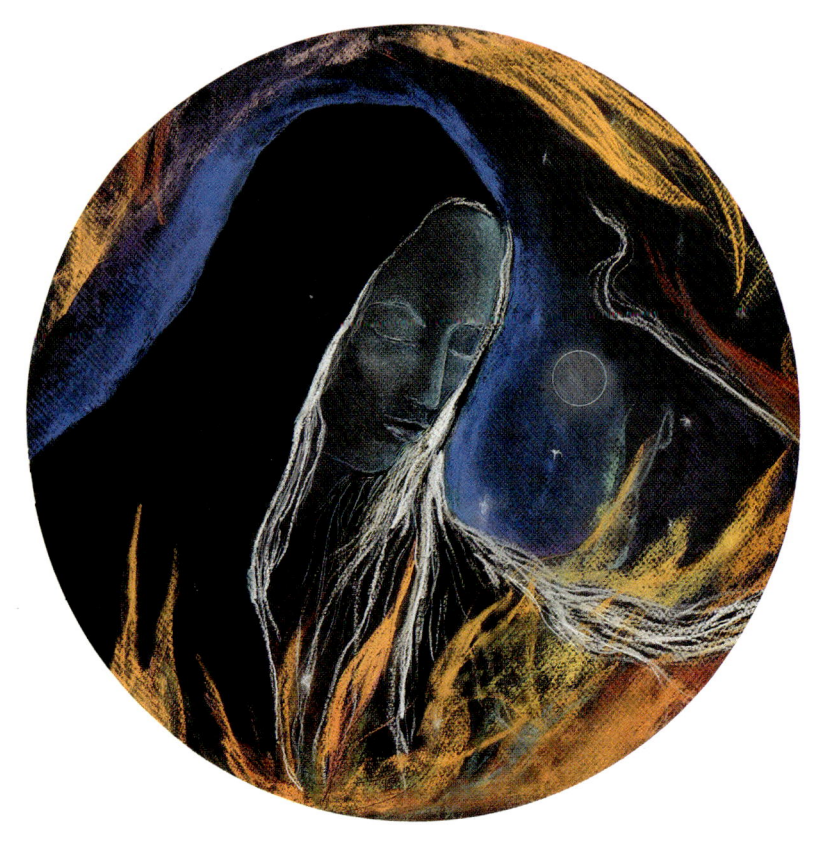

THE SOUTH

TABLE OF CONTENTS

INTRODUCTION	1
CALL FROM THE OLD ONES	9
THE WEST	15
Invocation	16
From the Old Ones	17
Crossroads: Movement into Change	18
West Exercises: I. Born of Water	21
II. Tears into Water	22
West Visualization: The Sea Journey	24
The Silver Thread I: The Story of Sea	27
The West Ritual: Hecate	38
West Invocation and Chants	40
THE NORTH	41
Invocation	42
From the Old Ones	43
Crossroads: Movement into Power	44
North Exercises: I. Into the Silence	47
II. Holding a Mountain	48
III. Into the Dark	49
North Visualization: The Heart of the Mountain	51
The Silver Thread II: The Story of Night	53
The North Ritual: The Ancients	72
North Invocation and Chants	75
THE EAST	77
Invocation	78
From the Old Ones	79
Crossroads: Movement into Vision	80
East Exercises: I. Beginnings	82
II. Faces of the Altar	82

    East Visualization: Dawn 85
    The Silver Thread III: The Story of Little Bird 87
    East Ritual: Taking Flight 100
    East Invocation and Chants 102

THE SOUTH 103
    Invocation 104
    From the Old Ones 105
    Crossroads: Movement into Voice 106
    South Exercises: I. Mirrors 111
                      II. Rage 111
                      III. Palms Upward 112
                      IV. Circle Energy 112
    South Visualization: Between the Flames 114
    Spiraling Outward into Power: From the Old Ones 117
    The Silver Thread IV: The Story of Rabbit 119
    South Ritual: Voices in the Fire 135
    South Invocation and Chants 137

APPENDIX 139
    Ritual 140
    Suggested Ritual Structure 140
    Clearing 141
    Grounding and Centering 142
    Smudging 144
    Casting a Circle with Stones 145
    Casting a Circle without Stones 146
    Invocation 146
    The Story 147
    Chants 147
    Dramatization 148
    Empowerment 148
    Returning Stones 148
    Grounding at the End of a Ritual 148

    Opening The Circle 148
    Celebration 149

THE OFFERING 150

NOTES 151

INTRODUCTION

THE MOON IN HAND is an invitation into the Mysteries and into ourselves. The journey is many journeys at once. It is a mystical journey into communion and oneness with all that is. It is also a personal quest of challenge, transformation and power. And it is a call from the Ancient Ones to honor the earth and all its inhabitants.

The Mysteries are the eternal sources of wisdom, power and peace. They are the truths we must have to live in fullness and harmony with oneself, others and the planet. They are truths once celebrated, practiced, and remembered by many peoples, but now overlaid with falsehoods of violence, exploitation, oppression, privilege and conformity. They exist in the spirit of ancient cultures. They exist also deep within ourselves and in the rest of nature. In journeying to those realms, we encounter change, healing, enlightenment and the power to act.

In our journey we meet the Ancient Ones—the keepers of the Mysteries—who weave them into patterns for each person's life. From all cultures and times, the spirits of those who have learned those truths welcome us and guide us and challenge us to dream our dreams and live in beauty.

The path of the journey is around the wheel of the Four Directions: North, East, South and West. We can enter the wheel at any direction. Each one is a passage of healing and power particular to that direction. We enter and re-enter, going around many times. Each journey brings us to a deeper and richer understanding of our own lives and our role in honoring the lives of all beings.

Each direction of the wheel is unique in its power. In my experience, the power of the North is the power of the Earth and of healing in darkness and silence. The power of the East is the power of air and the gift of vision and clarity. The power of the South lies in fire and passion that acts. The power of the West lies in water and the courage to change.

A woman whose beginning is in the East holds the gift of clarity and the ability to receive herself through her vision. The lessons of Air in the East will be the cord to her center.

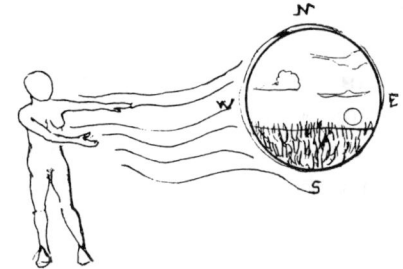

If she were to journey

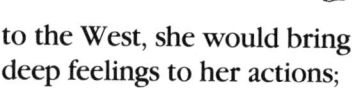

    to the South she would bring
will to her clarity, acquiring
the ability to act clearly;

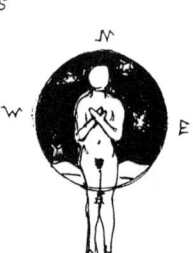

        to the West, she would bring
deep feelings to her actions;

    and

           to the North she would learn
to be still, to be silent.
She would bring wisdom to her
actions, learning when to act
and when not to act.

As each direction of the wheel is unique, each of us is unique in the way we receive the gifts of the Four Directions. We are individual wheels ourselves; we reflect the gifts we receive as we touch all with whom we come in contact.

To understand the power of the wheel we must understand our hearts. The heart is the center of the wheel, and it is with our hearts open that we learn to let go and make the journey. Human beings are the only animals given the gift to determine the course they will take. We are given the ability to question, to seek, to learn and to expand. When we develop our senses, we learn to go into a Silence, to hear and to touch. When we open our bodies as channels, we receive the ability to be and to feel. When we draw upon the Earth, we receive energy, allowing her warmth to flow through us; we become one with her and ourselves.

I

The wheel of the Four Directions is a vital religious symbol found in many Native American traditions, in ancient European traditions and now in the rebirth of Goddess traditions. It orders an earth-based spirituality that, in spite of genocidal efforts to stamp it out, has continued to survive.

Earth-based spiritualities grew out of an honor for nature, encompassing the fear and love for her power. In such traditions, Earth was seen as alive—healthy, nurturing and powerful. Natural law was sacred law. The communities learned from nature's rhythms, acknowledging them often as divinities. Birth and death became Sacred Mysteries. Value systems were based on the inherent value of Earth's forms: plant, mineral, element, animal, insect and human.

Today the exploits of capitalism and large social structures based on materialism and politics derived from systems of control have alienated us from Nature and her teachings. She, like the Native people of earth-based spiritualities, has been neglected, exploited, abused and destroyed.

Since childhood I have been drawn to this kind of spirituality. My parents left me when I was a child, and I was tossed from place to place by a bureaucratic welfare system. I soon discovered that the only constant in my life was nature. I had heard about Mother Nature, and longing for a mother, I adopted her as mine. I would lie down in the moss beds, feel her breath, hear her heartbeat and wonder at her beauty. I spent an enormous amount of time in the woods. I kept my experiences secret, afraid people would think I was strange. I read *Hiawatha*. Though it was written by a white man and stereotyped the people it described, it profoundly affected me with its beauty and the possibility of living with and from the land. I often "played Indian," as I called it then. Over and over I built shields and tried to heal my pain.

I also read the Greek myth of Persephone. I lived emotionally by the seasons, and with the light of spring, I was filled with celebration and magic.

As I grew older, I began to do meditations and simple rituals. Gradually the Ancient Ones came to me. They have been with me in times of crisis to enlighten, heal and empower me. They come from many cultures and from all over the world.

On one occasion, I was lying in the sun, meditating by a pond. By invitation, I was on sacred Indian ground. Before long, I left my body and found myself no longer near the pond on a sunny day but in the woods at night. There was only a little moonlight coming through the dark branches, lighting a path that led downward toward what looked like a body of water. As I followed the path, I came to a beautiful lake reflecting the moon, the sounds of gentle rhythms from small waves breaking on the shore. The scent of pine was very strong, and the overall feeling of the place was of overwhelming, peaceful sadness.

As I stood there watching the silhouettes of trees in the dark, I saw figures of women and men emerge silently from the trees. They surrounded me. I saw that they were the spirits of Indigenous people. They stared at me in silence. They continued coming from the trees; more and more joined the group that already surrounded me. The amount of power and sadness almost overwhelmed me as it poured from them into my body. I felt as if the encounter was never going to end.

At last, one man came out from the crowd and greeted me. We gestured to each other in a sacred way, and then he spoke, "We ask you with your work to acknowledge and return the honor which has been lost to the Indian spirit as it weaves through our many cultures. We ask you to make a vow to our Ancients."

I turned to all those who surrounded me that night at the lake and made a vow to them. I vowed I would honor and remember the spirits of the land as I traveled through my spiritual healing. With this the figures faded back into the trees, and once again I stood alone on the shore of the lake. I knew something very powerful had just occurred to me, and I had entered another realm of my power.

These are the words the people used that night at the lake. They referred to *the spirit* as one. I do not believe they meant a single Indigenous spirituality, but rather the spirituality of those who live with the earth and have been killed because of the depth of that relationship.

Since then, I have come to see the treatment of all races and classes, of many other groups of women and men and of the Earth herself as oppressive and violent. Although there are many differences and contradictions among the forms of oppression, all have been exploited, confined and mutilated, and in many cases, nearly eradicated.

In my spiritual journey now, I hear all their voices guiding my own quest for wholeness and power. I speak and write from an eco-feminist position. I am a witch, a lover of Mother Earth and Ancient ways, a shape bender, a rememberer of dreams, a builder of visions. I stand strong as a warrior against judgmental and prejudicial ideologies and practices. I seek the healing of the Earth and sustainable ways of living. As a witch I celebrate the pluralism and interchange of diverse spiritualities and cultures. The path to healing and power is not a single path but a web of paths, each one special and necessary, all connected and together resilient.

II

As I write about my connection with aspects of Native spiritualities, I am very much aware that white people have exploited, and continue to exploit, Indian spiritual practices. They are taken out of the context of the culture and community of which they are an intrinsic part. They are romanticized, individualized, trivialized and abstracted from a people's struggle for survival and the recovery of ancient ways. They are popularized as a single tradition, seen as "Native spirituality," as if the many nations on this continent all had a uniform culture.

And they are taken with no returning. They become still another way in which white people continue to profit from the lives of those they have tried to destroy. When whites write about and teach "Native spirituality," the prestige, honor, legitimacy and the money go to them, not to those who have suffered because of their deep spiritual commitment.

The question for me is "How can we who are white honor the wisdom in earth-based spiritual traditions without continuing such exploitation?" Certainly whites must become informed about the diversity of these spiritualities. On this continent alone, there are several hundred different Indigenous cultures. Each has its own complex and rich web of story, ritual and teachings.

Second, we have a responsibility to explore our own Euro-centric earth-based traditions for the resources in them. The rebirth of Goddess religion has enabled me to deepen that particular journey. It has also enabled and inspired me to be a part of the rebirth and rebuilding of a women's culture that honors and recreates some of that religion.

Further, honoring Native spiritual traditions means honoring peoples' struggles. For me, that means commitment to the ongoing struggle for self-determination and sovereignty through both legal means and direct action.

Finally, I think there is a critical difference between using symbols of different traditions when they profoundly connect with one's own inner being and when they are more superficially adopted. To pay enormous amounts for a weekend "experience of Native spirituality" is one thing and is easily exploitative. To descend into one's own core and connect with the voices and resources of many traditions reflects a different reality. To use the symbols that fit with that deeply spiritual journey is not exploitation but an honoring that transcends time and culture.

One day after a T.V. interview, I received a phone call from a very angry Native American man. He represented the Rhode Island Council of Indians. He accused me of exploiting tribal ways and threatened me. He told me they were to hold council at which I was to appear before 200 men. We talked for over two hours on the phone. We were able to share our sorrows and our love of Earth. I did *not* back off in the beginning when he threatened me. I remembered my earlier vision. The spirits that came to me in that vision were my "credentials," I told him. I do not question whether I am authentic or not. I struggle every day as a warrior. *Mother Earth does not discriminate by blood lines.* I believe our responsibility is to honor and protect Earth's spirit, to fight discrimination, exploitation and power over, and to break down barriers that separate our spirits. I believe that together—alive and powerful—we can and will rebuild a multi-faceted vision. In Ancient times, this vision was known and celebrated as the Goddess with a thousand names. To protect this vision and to be a part of this vision is my personal commitment.

When I shared my vision with him, I spoke from my heart. I told him how deeply I felt, and I shared the pain. It is where my teaching comes from. I wept the tears of the people whose ancient spirits heal in the trees, I wept the tears of the Earth. I wept the tears of the women who burned because they were witches. I wept the tears of the unborn children and the lost ones. He responded that he could feel I spoke from the spirit, and he gave me the honor of a new vision.

III

As I wrote above, this book is an invitation to a journey. The journey occurs in several ways—through invocations, messages from the Ancients, sharing our own stories, guided visualizations, rituals, exercises and children's stories. My hope is that each of these is like a facet of a diamond, illuminating dimensions of our struggles and opening us further to the healing power in the Mysteries and in ourselves as microcosms of that universe.

The book is designed primarily for group use, but it has many individual exercises also. When you use it alone, you may have to make a few adjustments. For instance, some of the exercises and visualizations call for closing your eyes; you will have to read them through first and then tape them or do them by memory.

The book is written to women. It can also be used by men or by women and men. Again, make the adjustments that are appropriate.

The content of the book is drawn from my own journey and work with ritual, the re-created Goddess heritage and the lives of women in my own cultural past, particularly those tried as witches. They are the sources of the many stories, symbols and images in the book that have become spiritually illuminating for me.

The book is organized around the Four Directions. Since my own most recent phase of the journey began with the West, I have begun the book there instead of the East, the place of beginnings.

Each section begins with an invocation. Read it and then pray it as you can. The invocation is followed by a message from the Ancient Ones and then a part of my own story. Ponder the message; think about its importance for your own life. After you have read my story, share your own, aloud to yourself or with the group. The exercises, visualizations and rituals are examples of what you can do in each direction, in each passage of the wheel. Not all may be equally relevant to your own situation. Draw on your experiences and the legacy of your spiritual, cultural and political traditions as I have drawn on what has been important to me. The word "create" comes from the word *crescent,* the crescent moon, changing moon, new moon—the shape of the moon that holds the potential. In other words, take the moon in hand and create.

The children's stories may come as a surprise to you. They are very important, however. I call them the silver thread that weaves. It weaved my own path together. When I lost my dreams and joy with many hard changes, I was called upon to return deep into the Mysteries, to journey into the North labyrinth to search for my innocence and in doing so to retrieve my hope. One evening as I went over my life, I found one simple thread in which I had weaved the intricate web of my spirit's path. It was the children's stories. It was a child—my spirit child—who became the weaver.

I sat down to write the East story of Little Bird. My spirit child was right there with me, leading me through this story. It seemed as if the spirit child in me knew the only way to reclaim hope or the ideal was to imagine it. By taking the foundation of the children's stories and manifesting in them the ideals in my life, I became inspired. Little Bird loved the sky and the moon and the stars. She saw the beauty in the simple. She saw the beauty in front of her, and she came to represent my ideals. I learned from her that The East is about recognizing the magic and believing in it!

I discovered that it is my spirit child who sees beauty unharmed. And I realized that it is the spiritual warrior in me who brings her beauty out to the world. The ideals in the stories brought balance to my spirit. They were healing to my inner child, and I believe that they will be to the children inside all of us. It is with this in mind that I have come to share these stories. If you want to know your path to power, ask your child to sit down and tell you a story that takes place "in the beginning of time, before time and after time."

You may wish to build a wheel with stones as a circle of energy for doing the exercises and rituals in this book and the many others you will create. To build it, find four stones, each one unique and connected with yourself, which will aid in the flow of power from the Four Directions. Go toward the horizon in the East, the place of beginnings, the power of air and enlightenment. Find the stone, listen to its song, bring it to your heart, give thanks and place it in the East of your Circle. As you stand facing the South, the place of fire and passion, will and action, find the rhythm of your body. Where does it wish to travel? Find your stone, bring it to your heart, give thanks and place it on the South of your circle. As you turn to the West, the place of introspection, water and change, search inside for what you seek, and the stone of the West will appear. Bring it to your heart, give thanks and place it on the Earth in the West of your Circle. Finally, turn to the North, where deep silence lies in the power of the dark, Earth and wisdom. Find your stone, bring it to your heart and place it in the North part of your circle.

As you sit in the center of this stone circle, rhythmic energy will flow into you and through you. You will find yourself in touch with the immanent life force. As you place your hands on the Earth within the Circle, Earth's heartbeat will become one with yours. You will feel the pulse, and as you search the skies, the universe will open, showing you this pulse is everywhere. It is the heart of all that is.

IV

I feel strongly that Earth is calling for all of us to respond. This book becomes one way I share my vision of the Ancient Ways. I believe when we share our stories, our power and our visions, our spirits transform. The sharing becomes a sacred act that empowers.

In honor, I acknowledge the Native people I met that day, the witches who died and all the women who held onto a vision. I invite you to go listen, place your ear on the Earth and hear the Ancients whisper their wisdom.

It is the Ancients who say, "When you are able to look into the eyes of your own spirit, you will come to see that you have been healed. And the eyes you are staring into you will recognize as the eyes of the future."

Blessed Be
Eclipse
August 21, 1990.

CALL FROM THE OLD ONES

Come, let us speak to you of the Sacred Wheel, the great circle of life, the path of the moon which radiates within and without. Let us speak to you of the Four Directions, the powers that flow toward our hearts, where we each hold our sacred mirrors.

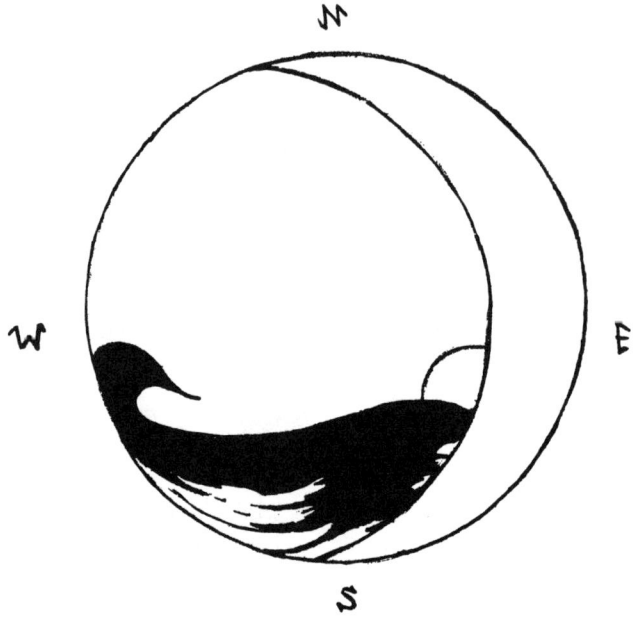

Let us speak to you of the West,
    the place of change,
    the place of courage to dare to look
    inward,
The West, where we search for our
    deepest feelings,
The West, where sunset splashes warm colors
    across our paths,
Where waves break, flowing into dark crevices.

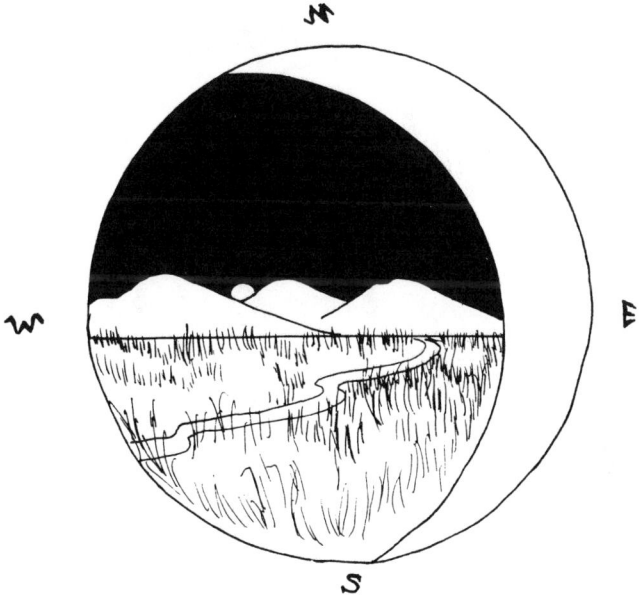

Let us speak to you of the North,
    the place of silence and wisdom.
The North, where we learn to stand still,
    regaining our power in the dark.
The North, place of dark blue skies,
    still winter nights,
White snow in the moonlight.

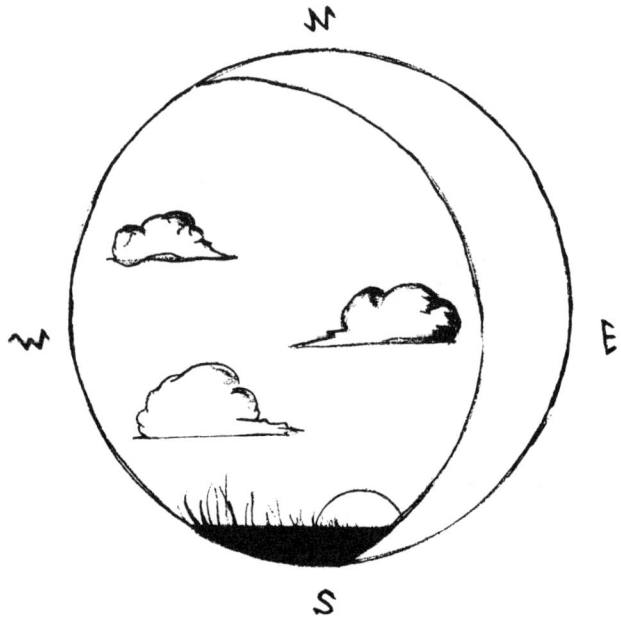

Let us speak to you of the East,
   the place of beginnings, dreams and clarity.
The East, where pale, wispy clouds
   welcome dawn.
Where the bird's flight streams forward
   as sparks of light.
The East, where our thoughts are refined.
Where the seed breaks through the earth,
   unfolding as a leaf.

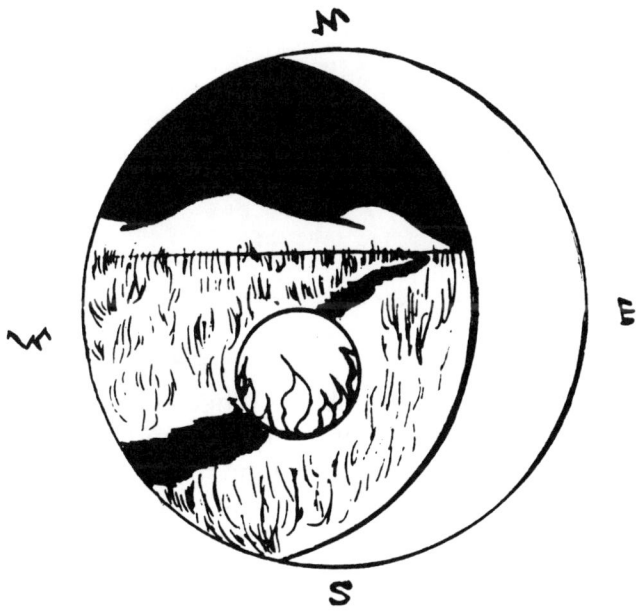

Let us speak to you of the South,
    the place of will, passion and desire.
The South, where the fire of our spirits
    dances in the midday sun.
Where the power to heal emerges.
The South, where the volcano erupts,
    oozing red lava over black stone.

Come travel many times around the Wheel, change, touch, learn. Learn to go into the Silence and call upon its power to bring a balance into your life. Learn the moon way, the circle way, the spirit way. Learn to stand at the crossroads and await the Ancients. Learn to be strong and patient. And in time learn the old way, the old way to hold the moon in hand.

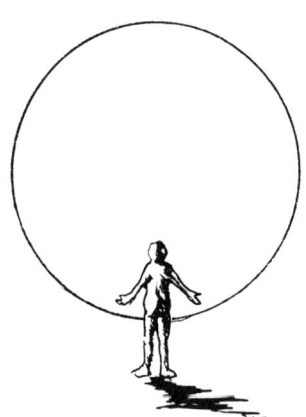

THE WEST

The place of courage, of daring to look inward.

INVOCATION

In the West,
> where the sun sets and we speak of change, of endings,
> where the Goddess saw her reflection in the sea
> and fell in love,
> where autumn returns, splashing red–orange hues
> on rhythmic waters,
> I flow.

In the West,
> where the Ancient One of change waits,
> I turn.

In the West,
> the place of courage, of daring to look inward,
> I search.

In the West,
> where deep feelings as still ponds reflect,
> I receive.

In the West,
> where waves break to return again as moontides,
> I heal.

In the West,
> where water flows as river's current,
> I follow.

GREAT POWERS OF THE WEST, I CALL UPON YOUR GIFTS TO BRING ME INWARD.

FROM THE OLD ONES

The Old Ones teach us that when we turn to the West, we welcome the cool autumn breeze and reach out to the fiery sunset before us. When we hear the leaves in full glory letting go of the branch, the voice of change seeps deep into our hearts. And when we turn to the sea to watch the waves breaking on cragged shores, thin streams flow into the crevices of our lives, redefining our boundaries.

It is in the West where the Ancient Ones call us to weave our deepest feelings into a web of stories. In the West the Goddesses Persephone, Inanna, Ariadne, Isis and other Ancient Ones call us to leave behind our securities and go in search of healing and power. We take the steps toward the dark womb of the earth. We find courage to go inward, to let go of the light, to follow the path toward the darkness into the Mysteries.

Often with fear we cling to what we know we must release. Courage is the gift of the West—courage to let go, courage to dare to look inward, courage to heal, courage to follow and to have faith. We search our very centers, we search for river's current and sea's tides, we search to become one with this flow. Like the river, we move onward to merge with the sea, to know the pull of the tides, to become the tide. When we let go and blend with these tides, the power of the West—the gift of courage—becomes ours.

All of nature teaches us the path of change when we stand in the West. We see the trees release their leaves, the fruit ripen to fullness, the bear lie down to rest. In the West the moon wanes to become the dark moon.

It is dusk when we stand at Hecate's crossroads. Hecate, Goddess of death and rebirth, leads us to our power. We reach out and take her gnarled hand, wrap our chilled bodies in her dark cloak and know we have become part of the turning of the Wheel.

As you stand in the West, feel the warmth of the fiery sunset as it slowly fades away. Let the courage of the Ancient Women who have gone before flow through you. Let go of that to which you cling to avoid change. Set it free, and with the depths of your spirit, come forward and touch the light of the moon.

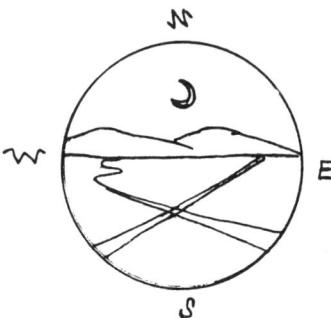

CROSSROADS: MOVEMENT INTO CHANGE

I was in a West passage of my life when I sat down to write this book. I was struggling through a very significant but painful relationship which I knew in my heart would end in sadness and tears. I also knew this ending would be part of my initiation through the West gateway into the Mysteries. This book became my thread through the labyrinths of empowerment. As the Goddess Ariadne had done, I weaved my way through dark and deep changes, spinning the unknown Mystery of my truth into everyday realities.

The West is a time when we learn the serpent's way. Like the snake, we shed our skins, letting go of old worn out ways. Shedding, I called out to the Goddess of change. Shedding, I called for courage to dare to look deeply into myself. Shedding, I journeyed to where depth and power merge inside me.

During this time of learning to let go and accept changes, I encountered an inner companion, known as Hecate, Old Wise One. The One who stands at the gateway of the West waiting calmly for us to come close. Moon sickle in hand, wrapped in her dark cloak, offering changes, she whispers to all who pass by, "Come, I will set you free."

One night she came to me in a dream. I stood there looking deep into her gray eyes. Her gnarled hand touched mine, and she drew me close to her. I was taken aback by her gentleness so clearly intertwined with her fearless power. Not for one moment did I forget that she was the Goddess of change, death and rebirth. I was afraid, but that night, I came to realize how deeply connected Hecate and I would become as I slowly moved into my power.

As I struggled with the relationship I knew was ending, I went into my past, into a tortured childhood. I remembered and re-experienced its confusion and loneliness, and I feared that leaving this relationship would send me once again into that pain and isolation.

One day, circumstances beyond my control caused me to turn and walk away from the relationship. That same day, a tremendous storm broke. The dark, thunderous sky reflected my sadness, fear and rage. As I stared out the window, I became one with the storm.

In a letter I wrote:
> The sky reflects our pain. Her rage is in the storm. But the storm is her way of letting go . . . . It is her tears, our tears that fall. These tears will flow to the river. The river will carry them to the sea, and the sea as the Mother will transform them into currents, waves and tides . . . .

As I cried with this storm, I recalled the courage of Persephone and the grief of Demeter. And I was both. I had descended into an underworld. I grieved for the relationship and for the self I would lose in that passage. For I knew I was embarking on a new path as I journeyed through the underworld.

As I saw my own experience in the larger context of nature and ancient myth, I began to understand what was happening in a new light. I found the courage to embrace the change, and I opened myself to the wisdom of the Ancients and eternal ways. One night Hecate, the Old Wise One, came to me. Wrapped in her dark cloak of a warm wave, she spoke to me, ever so slowly, "And now, my dear one, you too will wear the cloak of the Ancients."

It was many years before I understood what she meant, many years of learning about responsibility, of courage and change. But it began one stormy evening when I found the courage to let go, to turn toward the West passage of the Wheel and go in search of my power.

Death and rebirth are themes of many ancient myths. The power of transformation is central to these tales of descent to the underworld, in which goddesses confront gatekeepers and undergo trials before gaining power or accomplishing tasks. The stories tell of initiations, of facing our fears, dying to them, and then, in the very depths of the darkness, finding the power to heal.

The initiation may be prompted by many different crises at many different times in our lives. Mine was the crisis of a relationship. You may be confronted with the challenge to let go of a privilege—the privilege of being white or heterosexual in this culture for instance. Your challenge may be to let go of an accepted truth or ideal or goal. But whatever the occasion, it is an opportunity to follow the spiritual path of what I call the Ancient Ones, the path of profound transformation and power.

I encourage you to listen carefully to deep within, and if you do, you will hear the Ancients calling you, calling you to power.

WEST EXERCISE I: BORN OF WATER

Materials: Bowls of salt water
          A candle
          A full length mirror

A powerful exercise, preferably done with another person, but still meaningful alone, this is a simple ritual that connects us with the larger process. In this ritual focus on the power of water from the beginning of earth's early herstory to the present power of the waves breaking against the shore.

Sit or stand in front of a mirror. Give yourself time to stare into the mirror and see who you are. Mirror work is an outgrowth of a very ancient tradition of gathering power and learning tools for scrying (a method used to meditate). Water was often the original mirror into which women would stare deeply and wait for images to appear.

If you are doing this exercise alone, put a large bowl of water on the ground to allow you to cup water into your hands. If you are with another or in a circle, use a smaller bowl which can be held and passed around easily.

Sing or speak the following chant to help build a rhythmic flow of energy:

> *Born of water,*
> *cleansing, powerful,*
> *healing, changing,*
> *we are. (If alone, change to "I am.")*

This is to be repeated as many times as needed. Chants are most effective when given time to build into an energy form. They transcend singing the words to a song. With words, sounds and rhythms, they weave a web of energy filled with feelings, spiraling upward and outward.

As you become silent, pass the bowl of salt water. In turn, cup the water into your hands and focus on the powerful healing qualities of water. Feel how it can soothe you, how it flows, cleanses and cools.... Feel how it is connected to you and to all of life's creation....

Go back into the beginning of life; see how great oceans rolled across the surface of our planet... feel how, out of those bodies of water, life came! Also, see how the unborn is safe in the waters of the womb... feel the depths of a well... see refreshing streams... the power in a downpour... the healing in our tears... the breaking of waves... the dark tides at night. Choose the form of water which you see connected to you now. Are you raging? Like waves breaking? Are you turning inward as the tides? Maybe it is a time of peaceful reflection like a still pond. Whichever you choose, feel yourself connecting with its power.

Offer the bowl of water to yourself or your partner. Pour the water over your brow or your partner's, cleansing your face or hers, singing or saying the chant, "Born of water, cleansing, powerful, healing, changing, we are!" When the cleansing feels complete, bless some body of water special to you, pass the bowl to your partner to repeat the above, then pour the water onto the earth or into running water.

WEST EXERCISE II: TEARS INTO WATER

Materials: Two containers of water

Imagine a still, secluded pond with a smooth, flat surface. Leaning over the edge of this quiet pond is a solitary tree with one large limb stretched out over the water. As you stare at the tree, a leaf falls, turning into a tear as it lands on the still water. As the tear touches the pond, the water ripples in ever-increasing concentric circles.

Repeat this image of tears falling to the water until you see and experience a rhythmic flow of the circular ripples.

Place a bowl of clear, clean water in front of you. Stare at the water for a moment as it becomes still. Slowly let a few drops of water from another container fall into the bowl causing circular ripples. Then begin to pour the rest of the water slowly.

> See the water
> Hear the water
> Smell the water
> Taste the water
> Touch the water

Write down any impressions that come to you.

Feelings are one way we enter the path to the Mysteries. When we become vulnerable to another, when we open ourselves to the experience of the moment, we become like the leaf and the pond touching, creating ripples of energy flowing outward. Continue to pour water from bowl to bowl. Each time imagine that you are the water—pouring, flowing and changing.

Once again, sense the water as you pour it into the bowl, but this time, with your eyes closed. Feel the spirit of the water, hear its silence. Take a few minutes to be with the water. Letting yourself be with the water is a form of letting go. You become open to receiving the energy flow and learning your connection with the whole. Visualize what it is you need to let go of and release it!

Listen with your heart, and when you are ready, take this bowl of water and let it go to a body of running water—a river, the sea or a running drain.

WEST VISUALIZATION: THE SEA JOURNEY

Look into the water . . . see its clarity, its color, its rhythms. Listen for the voice of the water spirit and slowly close your eyes. Breathing deep into your belly, allow your body to relax as you exhale. Let all the tension drain from you as you begin to breathe in and out, slowly developing a rhythmic flow to your breath.

Breathe in and out, in and out, just resting behind the warm darkness of your eyelids while the spirit of the water radiates out to you.

The water is in the West, the place of introspection, of deep feelings. The West is the place of courage, of daring to look inward. The West is where the sun sets. Now, with the spirit of water surrounding you and as you rest evenly behind your eyelids, look over the horizon in the West as it meets the Sea. Watch the water as it gently rocks toward the horizon, pulling you toward the West. See how the sun begins to darken to deeper orange hues as it approaches the sea.

Feel the warmth of this nurturing light as it glows on the water, as the waves catch the flickers of light rhythmically . . . .

Breathe in and out in unison with the waves, taking in the power of the sun and the water . . . .

Feel your body as it relaxes into the waves, gently rocking back and forth . . . .

Now watch the sun as it sinks down into the soothing, massive waves; watch as it deepens in color to brilliant red, glowing as it slowly descends . . . .

See how the sun begins to turn color, see the sky in the background as it too changes . . . .

Feel your body descend towards the warm, welcoming water . . . .

The sun and your body are touching the water and slowly disappearing into the womb of the sea. Feel the surrounding water soothing you . . . .

Breathe in and out to the rhythm of the sea . . . .

Feel your body blend with the sea and slowly become the gentle rocking waves . . . .

Feel the water wooing you, soothing you, calming you. Let go, relax into the waves . . . .

Feel your power, your rhythm; feel the pull of the sea, feel the massiveness of your waves as they roll onward and outward . . . .

Now, as the sea, flow outward . . . .

You are the power of the sea; let it fill every part of your body . . . .

You are the tide; feel the pull, the depth, the cold, the warm surface . . . .

You are the power of the waves that break and reshape cragged rocks into smooth stones . . . .

Let your waters take you where they desire, maybe to a distant shore, to massive rocks of beautiful strength, or to the ancient wonders lying deep below the surface . . . .

Go gently in search of your gift that will appear. Let your heart guide you, teaching you the way of the West . . . .

(Allow several minutes to pass.)

Now, as you thank the sea, return slowly to the warm darkness behind your eyes. Feel the spirit of the water that continues to radiate from the sea, breathe it in and out, and when ready, touch the earth and return to the room, opening your eyelids slowly.

Take some time to record the journey, the images and feelings, the gift you received. If you are in a group, share some of your images and gifts. Begin to build a description of the West.

THE SILVER THREAD 1

                                  THE STORY OF SEA²

*In the West where the sun sets,
In the West, the home of the water.*

In the West, in the beginning of time, before time and after time, Sea reached out with great massive waves, straining toward the sky. With outstretched fingers of seafoam, grasping, pulling, searching, she called Thundercloud, "I want my daughter back! My daughter River!"

Her voice trembled in the dark as she called out. Her waves leapt upward casting shadows on the sand, but Thundercloud would not respond.

A long time ago, through sorrow and confusion, Thundercloud had gathered River into her darkness. And now she stood very dark, very still, hiding River.

In the quiet of the night, Sea rocked gently, softly singing a lullaby to her lost child.

One day in desperation, Sea traveled North,
  Where midnight and the stars remain;
  The North, home of Earth;
  Place of wisdom, of silence.
  In the North great mountains with deep crevices came close, touching Sea. Dark pines welcomed her as she rolled toward the shore.
  With a broken heart Sea cried out to Earth, "Earth, oh Earth, bring back my daughter River! Thundercloud stands still in the sky and holds her captive!"
  Sea began to weep.
  Earth heard Sea's tears and with her dark forest and tall mountains, came close and held Sea in her arms. She whispered, "My powers are to hold and to be still. I am here to nurture you, to make you strong. I do not have the power to take back River from Thundercloud."

A silence fell into Sea's heart as she listened to Earth's words. "Go see Air in the East; surely with her powers, she can help."

But when daylight came, Sea reached upward again and again, begging Thundercloud.

Thundercloud grew only darker. She had stolen River because she had felt empty and alone. In despair, she had drawn more and more of River into herself. What was once a roaring current lay now dry and bare. In her own way Thundercloud loved River, and she would not listen to Sea's pleas.

Sea's rage grew, and her waves crashed against the rocky shore as if she were trying to break her own pain. Her waves became cold, dark and threatening as they charged and withdrew again and again.

Despair began to penetrate the mist across the land. It was in the beginning of time, before time and after time. Sea had lost her daughter.

So Sea traveled onward to the East,
The East, where the sun rises;
The East, where dreams begin and clarity is found;
The East, home of Air.

As she approached East, she felt her massive waves lighten into ripples as they rolled toward the morning shoreline. Sun caps danced across her back, singing sweet notes of dreams. Air stood waiting, dressed in wispy hues of dawn.

"Air, oh powerful Air, Earth sent me saying you could help me with your great winds. My daughter, River, has been stolen by Thundercloud, who stands very dark and very still in the sky. She will not release her!"

Air listened carefully, blowing a gentle breeze around Sea to calm her tormented waves.

She looked up at Thundercloud and then back to Sea. She felt Sea's pain and saw Thundercloud's ominous strength. She thought for a long while.

"*Dear Sea, I have great winds; this is true,*" *she said. "I can blow Thundercloud away or bring her close, but I can't take River away from her. Go seek Fire in the South. Maybe she can help.*"

Sea turned toward the South, leaving behind the gentle breeze of East. Her currents flowed toward the great powers of the South;

The South, where one finds midday and hot sun;
The South, home of spirit, home of Fire.

As she arrived, she felt the warmth of Fire's flames. She heard their crackling as they leapt in front of her. She felt her currents deep inside swirl and dance as she stood there in front of this spirit, Fire.

The flames grew to amazing heights, sparkling in the sky, as Fire bellowed across the water, "I am Fire! I am the power of will! I have the power to act. To take what I want. To leave what I wish."

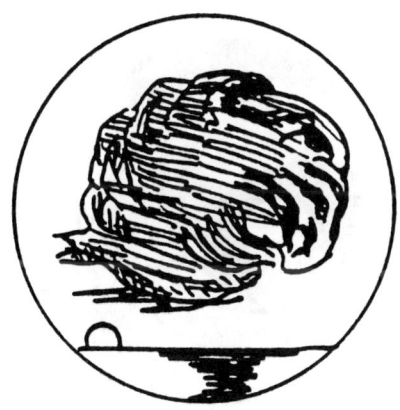

"Yes, I can take River back from Thundercloud! But I cannot bring her to you safely. It is the gift of all our powers that will bring River home.

"Dear Sea, you must turn inward to the power of your tides. You must follow the ways of your mighty waves breaking.

"Thundercloud in her time will fill to her shape, and in time I will act!

"Now dear Sea, return to the moonlight, go inward. Call upon your power to turn."

So Sea, with massive waves, moved away into the darkness; she knew her time had come to turn inward to the deep.

Soon the only sound in the night was her waves as they rolled onto shore, breaking, pulling and pushing the sand as it glittered in the moonlight.

Over and over she could hear her heart beat and feel her body pulsating in the rhythms of her slow moving waters as they danced to the moon.

In the dark she touched her pain, and through her tears she could see her currents and the waves that bulged and let go, breaking, releasing, helping her to see the power of change, the power of returns. And as her waves reached up to the moonlight, Sea came to understand that her power was reflected in every thing she did, in the movements of her waves, the pull of her currents, the salt in her tears. Hers was the power to know that all things change and all things return! It was hers to know that all returns to the Mother. With this knowledge deep inside her, Sea turned inward and became the ever-changing, ever-returning tide.

And as Sea came into her power, Fire saw the time had come. She called the great powers together. They all came close to Sea as they watched Fire become very silent. Sea watched intently as Fire gathered all her power into one force—and only as Fire can do, with a flash of a moment, changed time with one powerful act.

Suddenly from her outstretched flames, a bright, large shimmering lightning bolt leapt upward, piercing Thundercloud's darkness!

What had been pain was opened.

What had been fear was scattered.

What had been mystery took shape.

Through the opening, River, a brilliant rainbow serpent, slithered downward, spiraling faster and faster down into Earth's arms.

River was a torrent—spiraling, rushing forward, running wild in pain, grasping at the trees, the bank and any stone close by. Her body roared against Earth like the sound of many storms unfolding. Her voice was weeping as she reached for the rocks and the trees to slow her down.

She called for help as she heard Sea's voice in the distance. Each tree and rock that tore away felt her pain as she called out. A weeping sound filled the air as they heard the voice of River.

Fire burned brightly, lighting the dark sky for River's path.

Air came with gentle winds, soothing her surface.

Earth moved her body close, gently guiding River.

Soon in the warmth and strength of Earth's body, River quieted down. In the stillness of the night, she began to flow, to find her home.

And there, waiting with open arms for her return, were the tides of Sea's heart.

WEST RITUAL: HECATE

INTENTION

This is a ritual to search through our lives and see where we need to change and let go. Where do we need Hecate to come with sickle in hand and help us to cut away the bonds that bind us? In this ritual we each become the serpent shedding our skin. We also become Hecate as we invoke change. Hecate is very powerful, and it is important, therefore, that each of us be prepared for changes to come into our lives. So a discussion might be needed prior to the ritual for those who choose not to work with such energy.

MATERIALS NEEDED

    Smudging, sage and shell
    An altar in the center
    Bowl of water
    Candles, enough for each woman. Four larger candles for the four directions, placed on the altar in the center.
    A bell
    A drum
    Rhythm instruments

CLEARING (see Appendix)

GROUNDING AND CENTERING (see Tree of Life exercise in Appendix)

SMUDGING (see Appendix) A chant of "snake woman shedding her skin" can be sung.

CAST CIRCLE (see Appendix) Light the four-directions candles. With the circle cast, each woman lights a candle one at a time from the woman next to her.

INVOCATION (see Appendix)
CHANTS "Snake woman," Hecate chant, "We all come from the Goddess". Use one drummer in the Hecate chant to keep the rhythm. Too many drummers can add a variety of rhythms, confusing the slow, methodical beat that builds the energy.

STORY (see Appendix) The Story of Sea.

DRAMATIZATION (see Appendix) While chanting the Hecate chant, each woman should focus on what she wishes to let go of in her life. She asks to see where her fears and pain have been. She may ask herself questions about where she feels blocked or depressed or where she has been afraid to change.

One woman, who serves as Hecate, enters the circle with the bowl of water, asking the circle, "What is it you release? What do you dare to change?" She lets the words come to her as she channels Hecate. Then one at a time she goes to each woman, stares into her eyes and asks her to let go. Each woman, when ready, puts out her candle in the water and welcomes Hecate into her life. (If a woman is not ready to welcome Hecate into her life, she can blow out her candle, sending the light outward into time.)

Hecate extinguishes the four-directions candles.

EMPOWERMENT The room has become totally dark, and the chanting has softened until there is silence. Wait a minute or so, then one woman rings a bell and begins the chant:

> *We all come from the Goddess*
> *And to her we shall return*
> *Like a drop of rain*
> *Flowing to the ocean.*

Allow the chant and energy to build while women join in with their instruments, using harmony and sea sounds. Then one at a time, relight the four-directions candles as the energy builds to a cone of power.

GROUNDING (see Appendix)

RETURN STONES (see Appendix)

OPEN CIRCLE (see Appendix)

CELEBRATE (see Appendix) Feasting, dancing and/or singing.

INVOCATION TO HECATE

Ancient Mother, whose heart holds the unborn and the lost one, hear me.
Wise One, bring me deep into the darkness of your cloak, where I may find silent rest.
Aged One, I reach for your gnarled hand that stretches across time, guiding me to a distant crossroads where you wait alone in the ashes of your flames.
Ancient One, your voice is the sound of the blackbird's wing against my back.
Your song is the violin against the chill of Autumn winds.
Aged and weathered, your grayed eyes stare into my soul, And I feel your promises luring me to let go.
Oh Hecate, great Mother of the Ancients, still my trembling.
Come to me.

WEST CHANTS[3]

Snake Woman

Snake woman shedding her skin,
Snake woman shedding her skin,
Shedding, shedding,
Shedding her skin.

Starhawk

Hecate[4]

Ancient queen of wisdom,
Hecate, Hecate,
Old one, come to us.

Sparky T. Rabbit

We All Come From The Goddess[5]

We all come from the Goddess
And to her we shall return
Like a drop of rain
flowing to the ocean.

Z. Budapest

THE NORTH

The place of wisdom, the power to be silent, to be still;
The home of the Ancients;
The power of the dark, the heart of Earth.

INVOCATION

In the North,
> the place to be silent, to be still,
> where the blood of the Ancient Ones flows through my
> veins, I gather my wisdom.

In the North,
> I build my shield, dance my path onward.

In the North,
> I learn the power of darkness
> and welcome the gift of light.

In the North,
> where trees no longer bend, but wait,
> where Demeter in frozen silence grieves,
> I come to gather in the dark, to touch my truth.

In the North,
> the falling snow touches my sense of silence,
> the barren land brings me close to the hearth.

In the North,
> where the mountain carves her shape, silhouetted across
> the midnight sky,

In the North,
> the wolf's cry spirals through me
> reminding me of the power of the Ancients' call at
> midnight.

GREAT POWERS OF THE NORTH, I CALL UPON YOUR GIFTS TO STILL MY HEART WITH YOUR WISDOM!

FROM THE OLD ONES

The Old Ones teach us that as we journey, we need a place to rest, to heal. In the North we come to such a place. In the North the power comes into our lives to teach us. In the North we learn to stand still, to be one with the Earth and the Universe.

The North, as each direction, has its own unique gift of beauty. The dark, winter, midnight skies, stillness, silence—these are all the reflections of the North. The North power is like the dark, warm womb, where a human spirit evolves safely and securely.

It is in the moment before birth, in the darkness of the North, that we come to know ourselves. More than in any other direction, we go into the Silence, to hear the rhythm of our lives, the thread that weaves beyond time and before time.

Find your sacred place, whether it be a quiet room, a corner, or a forest. Find a place where you can align yourself with the midnight sky. Find the star that radiates from your center. Open yourself to this star and see how—out of this gift of darkness—a form unfolds, alive and powerful, growing and evolving, and know that what is evolving is the vision, the soul of the unborn.

Come stand in the North as a tree in winter, bare but strong. Remember the roots that burrow down into the dark to find strength and power to sustain it through the winter chills. Become the tree whose branches reach high up to the universe but whose foundation is deeply planted in the Earth.

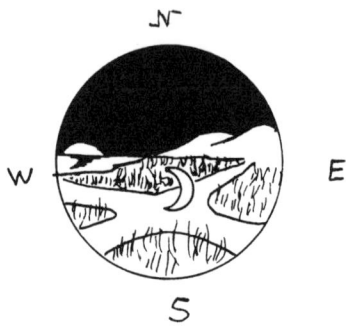

CROSSROADS: MOVEMENT INTO POWER

As I journeyed through the West passage, changed jobs and lost a relationship, I found myself deep in the crevices of my inner labyrinths. My life fell apart and I moved into the North. Dark mazes through the Mysteries lay ahead of me. I held onto the book I was writing. I felt driven to write. I felt it was one way I would heal myself and Earth. The path to my healing and Earth's healing became one and the same. I heard the incessant beat of Earth's heart, telling me She was alive but trembling, telling me She found no peace. The heartbeat told me there was a harshness, a rage that ran throughout Her body.

Earth called out. Through her struggles and my own, the Ancients were holding council with me, guiding me into power and healing, teaching me to become a voice for Earth. I tried to hold on to this book I was writing. I knew that writing was one way to heal myself and the Earth. But for a long time, I remained afraid and powerless.

One day I called a counselor friend. I ranted and raved to her that this spiritual process was all crazy and probably didn't really exist; that even if it did, I was tired and drained and depressed and didn't want to have anything to do with it! I was panicking. I knew I was about ready to encounter new challenges related to empowerment.

My friend supported and believed very strongly in my spiritual quest. She said she would keep the memories, images and experiences for me, and when I was ready, she would be there with them.

She became my dear Ninshubur, the woman in the myth of Inanna who waited and held onto the memories while her queen, the Goddess, descended into the underworld to meet her sister Ereshkigal.

Those words calmed me and left me free to do nothing but be still with my silence.

One winter day not long after that time, I went for a walk in the woods. Something beckoned me to these woods. From experience, I knew this particular feeling to be the call from the land below. I also knew to follow this yearning whenever it appeared because it would bring me farther down my path.

The snow was knee high, and it was a strenuous walk to an old circle I had made the spring before. Four trees still marked the now hidden stones. In the center of the stones, I sat and stared at the dark, bare branches etched against the brilliant blue sky. I felt myself connect with the trees, and soon I found myself following their roots deep into the dark, moist soil. I heard the trees whisper, "Our roots grow deep, come hold onto these roots."

As I breathed deep into my belly, relaxing into a meditation, I began to call upon the Ancients, asking and begging for help with the sadness I was carrying inside. I missed my lover's warmth and comfort; I remembered the gentle summer breeze when we had built this stone circle. I remembered the hope we had together, and most of all, I remembered the dreams we created. Now I could feel how deeply alone and lost I was. My tears just kept falling on the cold, clean snow.

The Ancients did not respond, and I went deeper into meditation. After a long silence, I heard a voice, like a heartbeat, deep and resounding through me, "You are one of us! You are an Ancient. Don't you know this?"

I didn't want to know this, nor did I care. My grief was too overwhelming. My only response was, "No, not now; I will deal with that later."

Nothing else was said, and after awhile, I came back to the present, chilled and ready to go home.

As I opened my eyes, there in the stark white snow lay a black wing fanned upward. It had not been there when I sat down, and I knew it was a sign and a gift from the Ancients!

I took the black feathers with me and decided to build a staff symbolizing my connection with the Ancients. I started to look for just the "right" stick, picking up different ones as I walked by them. I came across one stick that felt right, but I decided it didn't look right, so I left it behind. By the time I reached the car, I had not found the "right" staff, and I knew it really was the one I had left behind in the woods. Although I was tired and it was late, I trudged back through the snow to find the one stick I had dropped.

I found it, and when I picked it up, I began to feel this incredible surge of energy. I crouched, ready to leap forward at any moment, each muscle in my back tensed and powerful. I felt wild and powerful, a white tiger, hunting her prey ever so slowly. I stalked the woods, staff in hand. I leapt forward and was transformed into a hawk with outspread wings, soaring above the trees! And then I was wild and free, running in the snow as a wolf. I heard the rhythmic sound of my panting. I ran and ran until I felt ancient, as if time had shifted, and I were a part of that shift. I invoked the Goddess Diana and became the wild one, the hunter, the protector of the woods. I was strong and brave; I felt good and I welcomed the energy that flowed through me.

I have kept those feathers, and I place one on my staff each time I take a major step into my power.

This experience in the woods—the wing, the Ancients' message, my feeling so alone, depressed and confused, my going back into the woods—this is North work. The North is where I learn to accept the power that comes to me as I journey along my path. It is a place where I come to respect the Ancients' way of teaching me to reclaim my power.

NORTH EXERCISE I: INTO THE SILENCE [6]

It is time to touch the Silence, to become one with nature and other people. When we go into the Silence, we learn to hear the rhythm of the great Mystery, the heartbeat of Earth.

Going into the Silence, we learn to be alone with our thoughts:

> *To hear the Silence*
> *To listen and to see the Silence*
> *To listen and to taste the Silence*
> *And, with closed eyes, to feel the Silence.*

It is in quiet moments that we find our heartbeats. When we let go and search the dark warmth of our silence, we feel the rhythmic beat of the Earth vibrating, flowing toward us.

Sit in a quiet, still place, preferably outside. Allow yourself to become comfortable and relaxed.

Breathe the energy of the surroundings deep into your belly, then release the air and all lingering tensions. Let the beauty of the trees, the sky, the earth come deep inside you as you slowly breathe in and out. Let the worries of your life slip away. Allow the rhythmic flow of your breath to meet your surroundings. Give thanks to the presence of nature and make an offering of flower petals, tobacco, a special stone or whatever seems right. The symbolic gesture of making an offering is a way of speaking to nature, of saying: "This is a part of me, and I offer it to you in thanks."

Acknowledge the Four Directions, their powers and their presence. Acknowledge the sky and the Earth and give thanks. With these acts you have created a protective circle of energy flowing around you and to you.

If this exercise is new to you, find an object nearby: a stone, a small tree, a flower or a blade of grass. Find one object on which to rest your eyes. Remember that everything in the woods has a spirit. Let the image of the object fade in and out of focus as your eyes remain open.

Listen to the sounds around you; taste the air and touch the ground. Close your eyes and go behind your eyelids to the darkness, the soft, warm darkness of yourself. Breathe in and out as you let the darkness flow; then slowly open your eyes. Gently focus on the object again, examining its shape, color, size and texture. Carry the image of the object inward as you close your eyes again.

Allow the image to settle in front of you just behind your eyelids. As you become comfortable with it there, go deep inside toward your center. Open a path for your warm, dark energy to flow to the object, to connect with it.

When you feel your self flowing from your center to the image of the object behind your eyelids and when you feel comfortable with that flow, focus again on the image of the object. With your eyes still closed, allow yourself to become completely silent and open. Listen to the voice, the spirit of the object; listen to its heart. Open yourself to touch, experience, and learn the special gift from the Earth. Listen to the voice. Rest with this presence for a while.

Now begin to listen for the heartbeat of your object. The rhythmic heartbeat endures in each of nature's objects. Join the heartbeat of this object, stay with the rhythm for a few minutes as it flows in and out. Give thanks to the object and allow your warm, dark energy to return slowly to your center.

When you feel ready, touch the ground and slowly return to your surroundings. Look downward as you re-enter the present, so you won't be jolted when you finally open your eyes. Look at the object in front of you. You and this object have connected spirits. When you feel the need again, you can return to this place of sharing nature's rhythm. You can choose at any time to go into the Silence, whether it is with one object or many, whether it is to connect with a group, sense the energy of a landscape, or spend a quiet moment with a person or other animal. With time and experience, you can learn how to flow in and out of the silence effortlessly. The process is then no longer an exercise but rather a way of being, a part of your life.

NORTH EXERCISE II: HOLDING A MOUNTAIN

Materials: Three stones

The mountain is the earth's altar, raised to the sky; each stone, tree, flower and river becomes this mountain. If I pick up a stone from this mountain, what I hold in my hand, symbolically, is the mountain. If I stand far away, I see the mountain's shape. To take on the power of the North is to be able to hold the stone in your hand and see the shape of the mountain.

You can learn to do this by starting with three stones. Take the three stones and cup them in your hands. Feel their edges as they touch you, as they touch each other. Listen to the sounds they make together as you rub them and shake them. Open your hands and see them touching; smell them; taste them . . . .

Now close your hands and eyes and feel the stones' energies. The stones collectively have a powerful energy, and each stone separately is powerful.

Write down any images or impressions that come to mind. Ask, "Where else in my life do I experience collective power? Individual power? How do they reflect each other? How do I reflect them?"

Now hold one stone at a time. Touch it, listen to it, see, feel and taste it . . . .

Now hold two stones at a time. Feel their differences . . . feel their sameness . . . feel their connections with you.

This is the silence the stones reflect. Opening yourself to two stones brings you to the place of "being still," the place of the North.

Hold one stone in each hand and allow the stones' energies to bring balance into your body as the energy flows from either side. The power of the North is found in the connecting energy between differences. This cannot be found intellectually. It must be sensed. Go into the Silence with the stones.

Add the third stone, the top stone. See what it feels like to have many energies flow through you at once.

Do this exercise often. Increase the number of stones you hold each time. Soon you will begin to know the power of holding a mountain in your hand.

NORTH EXERCISE III: INTO THE DARK

Materials: A cauldron or large bowl of stones
          Flower petals, corn meal or tobacco for an offering

In this exercise you should be in darkness in a quiet place, preferably outside, otherwise in a room with no light. Have a cauldron or bowl of stones, corn meal, flower petals or tobacco with you.

Sit very still. Concentrate on quieting yourself by taking deep, long breaths. Begin to focus on the stillness, listen to the silence with all your senses. Let it totally surround you.

Stand and notice the direction you feel physically drawn to. Go toward that direction. When you have come to the place that is calling you, find the stone that awaits you there. Bring it to your heart, give thanks and make an offering of flower petals, tobacco, corn meal or whatever gift you choose. This stone will hold the power of the North. Be with your stone, go into the Silence with it. Give thanks to the earth. Bless her body.

If you cannot be outside, search for the stone in the bowl. Allow your hand to rest just above the bowl. Feel the energy radiate out up to your hand. See which way it is pulled, follow that energy, touch the stones until your hand connects with one. Give thanks.

NORTH VISUALIZATION: THE HEART OF THE MOUNTAIN

Close your eyes and remain behind the warm darkness of your eyes....

Breathe deep into your belly, allowing yourself to relax. Let all of the tension drain slowly away as you develop a rhythmic flow to your breathing.... Breathe in and out again and again, in and out until you find yourself relaxing into a comfortable dream state....

Imagine yourself standing in your spirit land on a wide open plain.... Sense the silence of this landscape as night begins to fall.... As you gaze at the evening sky and outstretched land, you become aware of a throbbing and bulging in the earth. You begin to hear and feel a rhythmic pulse.... Slowly a massive mountain begins to emerge and take form in front of you. It grows upward and stretches outward into the dark sky....

Breathe in this power of emergence.... Feel the ancient energy of the place as it pushes the mountain upward into the dark night.... Feel the Mother giving birth through the soil... When the earth is no longer pushing, see how this mountain becomes a part of the silent landscape.... Feel the rhythms of the night as they flow toward you.... Breathe in and out, allowing this life source to come into you.... See it and feel it as the warm and fertile power of the dark.... Feel its healing energy as you breathe in and out.... With each breath, feel your own strength growing....

In the dark, feel the Earth beneath your feet growing, alive and surrounding you like the safe warm arms of a mother.... Smell the deep woods, the pine needles, the moss and fern, the moist dampness of the soil.... Breathe it all in, feeling the magic of the woods as it surrounds you.... See the crisp clean air as the twinkling stars shine through the shadows of the trees....

Climb the path leading upward to the top of the mountain. As you reach the top, find a clearing, a comfortable place to lie down and gaze up at the stars.... See how brilliant and clear the night sky is. Breathe in the expansive feeling of the universe.... Find one star that is particularly special to you and align yourself with it....

Imagine you are directly in line with a light coming from it. Breathe in this light . . . .

As you continue to breathe, begin to relax your body into the darkness of the Earth, feel your body sinking deep into the mountain . . . . Move through the Earth, deep into the root systems . . . deep into the wetness . . . deep into the stones and shale . . . . Continue and go deeper and deeper into the center . . . . See the remains of old relics . . . . Imagine how they were once a part of an ancient civilization . . . . Breathe in the energy of the ancient relics and bones of old ones . . . . Continue, feel the pulse of the Earth . . . the pulse of time . . . the pulse of life . . . . Feel the pulse growing stronger and louder until you have come to the core of the mountain, the heart of Earth . . . the realm of the Ancients . . . . Breathe in this power, knowing it is a part of your being . . . .

Ask the Ancients to come close . . . .

Ask the Ancients to speak to you . . . .

Listen to what they say . . . .

(Allow a few minutes to go by).

Now it is time to return to the warm darkness behind your eyes. When you are ready, return through the earth and back to where you began this journey. With your hands gently tap the ground and give thanks to the Earth. Open your eyes feeling well and alive. Write down any important images or messages that came to you during this journey.

THE SILVER THREAD II

THE STORY OF NIGHT

Night came lonely and scared, her face drawn and tired. Her dark cloak remained tightly wrapped around her body.

Night had lost her way, and no one could guide her back home. She roamed the land searching, longing for rest and comfort. But the small creatures ran and hid as she appeared, and the great predators stood very still in her presence.

It was the beginning of time, before time and after time.

 Night felt so alone and empty. Her only source of comfort was the sweet, gurgling voice of River as she flowed onward to distant lands. In exhaustion, Night lay down next to River and cried out, "River, oh soothing River, help me. No one comes close to me, for I am Night; I am darkness; I am of the Mysteries. All seem to fear me."
 She began to weep, "I am lost, and I have no gift to offer."

River heard Night's pleas and felt her despair, which had begun to spread across the land. With compassion River responded, "Follow me, follow my flow to the West." The soft notes of flowing water were the only sound in the dark, soothing Night, wooing her to follow.

Night gathered up her cloak and followed River's path through the forest and across the land to the West, home of Sea. In the West, Sea came crashing with her ominous waves across the deserted shore, grasping for the silvery sand. Night felt a mysterious power as the sea mist surrounded her while the thunderclap of waves broke in front of her.

"Sea, oh powerful Sea, I am Night. I have lost my way and I have no gift. My despair is spreading across the land!"

Sea listened, her waves calming to a rhythmic flow as she answered Night's pain with a lullaby. In time she replied, her voice rising above the waves, "I am keeper of the West, the place of introspection, courage and deep feelings." Her voice became low and solemn. "I will bring you to your depths, but I cannot lead you home nor give you your gift." Night listened, and deep in her heart she knew Sea spoke the truth. "I can offer you courage to look inward, but it will not take your loneliness away," said Sea.

Night knew her stillness belonged elsewhere as Sea spoke, "It is time for you to leave. Your darkness makes my waves dark and awesome, and soon all will fear me and become lost in your darkness!"

Night turned away, leaving Sea behind her in the West. A brilliant sunset splashed across Sea's back, and ripples rolled outward as she whispered, "Night, my beautiful Night, take my gift of courage for your travels. Keep it close to your heart and go seek Wind in the East. The East, the place of beginnings, clarity and dreams."

    Night traveled for a long time and finally came to a meadow where tiny spring flowers with crystal dewdrops greeted her. Her eyes filled with tears as she saw their gentle beauty, and she reached out to touch them. But as she came close, they were chilled by the winter-like darkness and withdrew. She sat down, wrapped her dark cloak around her and wept. Once again, she felt the depth of the pain of her loneliness.

Soon the trees answered her tears with a wind song. Their leaves rustled and swayed as they chanted, "Return, return great Night to your home. Return, return."

But Night was lost and did not know where her home was. She cried out above the chanting, "I am Night, I have lost my way and have come to see Wind!"

As she spoke, a gentle breeze soothed her brow and dried her tears. She could feel the light touch of Wind against her soft cheeks. For a moment her pain quieted, and she listened carefully to the notes of the Wind. "I am Wind. I am the song of your heart."

Night smiled as she listened. "It is the melody of beginnings that guides you through your passage. I cannot give you your gift, but the power of my song is heard in the flute of ancient times. It speaks of your gift, your power and your beauty."

Night heard the flute and began to dream. She wanted to rest in the East, but Wind caressed her body and pushed her onward. "Take my gift of dreaming and bring it into your heart. Let it guide you to the South, the home of Fire, the place of the spirit."

 So once again Night turned away, and as she left, she saw behind her the pastel colors of dawn and the sweet spring flowers opening to the new day.
 Night headed toward the South, where Fire waited. Warmth and brilliant passion filled the air, tingling through Night's body, pulling her onward with great speed. She felt the gifts of Wind and Sea merge and flow through her core as she approached Fire.

    The passion of her dreams grew in her heart, and her courage surrounded her as she stood facing Fire.
    Fire's flames crackled and leapt upward touching Night as sparks of passion. Her voice became powerful and strong as she spoke, "I am Night. I have come for your help."

"And I am Fire," Fire's voice bellowed through the flames. "I have waited a long time for you to come close to me."

Night remained silent.

Fire continued. "My power is of the spirit, of will, of expanding light. And yours is of deep darkness, of wisdom, of the power to be still." Night listened, standing still and very strong as Fire spoke.

Night opened her cloak of darkness and spread it across the land. Fire answered with her flames, "Come, come join me in the dance of life." Night came forward. And for a moment Light and Dark were equal in power and beauty.

　　Time passed and Fire turned to Night saying, "It is time for you to go home. You have journeyed far, and it is in your home you will find your rest. Turn away from me and follow the path to the distant mountains of the North." Night turned away and Fire lit her path as she moved onward toward the dark mountains that awaited her.

    In the North the cool, crisp air livened her body, and she hurried onward, her dark cloak trailing behind her. As she advanced, the forest greeted her. The snow-capped mountains opened their arms, welcoming her. She climbed the tallest mountain, and as she reached the top, she breathed in the power of the North. She felt the power rush through her. She held close the gifts of the West, East and South.

Night knew she had found her home. An inner calmness grew as she lay down to rest on top of the mountain. Night was at peace. She had found her home and waiting there was her gift—

the Moon.

NORTH RITUAL: THE ANCIENTS

INTENTION

This is a ritual to claim our power and connect to the Ancients.

MATERIALS NEEDED

    Smudging, sage and shell
    Large stones to build the base of a mountain
    Smaller stones and sacred objects
    Candles and candle holders, enough for everyone in the circle
    A base of dirt, sand or similar material for building mountain, which will serve as an altar
    A hand mirror
    A bowl or cauldron of ashes made from burnt sage, lavender and pine or any other group of herbs. These ashes should be ground into a fine powder
    Moss, leaves, straw, flower petals, all natural material for covering the mountain
    Drum and rhythm instruments

THE ALTAR The altar is built before doing the ritual. If it is inside, a large cookie sheet or piece of plywood may be used for a base, on which wet sand or earth is formed in the shape of a mountain. Moss is a beautiful material to cover the mountain, but leaves and grass work. In the dirt or sand, place a few branches to look like trees. Use little stones to build paths—have fun, be imaginative. On the top, place a hand mirror that can be used during the ritual. Bring sacred objects—little animals, goddesses, crystals—and place them on the mountain.

    Place candles in candle holders around the base, along with the Four-Directions candles.

CLEARING

GROUNDING AND CENTERING

SMUDGING "Ancient Mother" may be sung while smudging.

CASTING A CIRCLE

INVOCATION "Persephone, Queen of the Underworld" or "Charge of the Goddess".

STORY The Story of Night or another of your choice

CHANTS "Ancient Mother," "Goddess Medley."

DRAMATIZATION Building a Mountain

Before the ritual begins, each woman chooses a stone as her contribution to building the mountain. She has the stone next to her as she sits in the circle. All begin singing softly, with one drummer to set a soft consistent rhythm:

> *Isis, Astarte, Diana,*
> *Hecate, Demeter, Kali,*
> *Inanna.*

As everyone sings, one person at a time goes to the altar and raises a stone and stares into the mirror. She turns to the women in the circle and tells them when in her life she has felt powerful. Then she places her stone on the mountain. She lights a candle and returns to the circle. The next woman takes her turn. When everyone is finished, build the energy with chanting and instruments until it rises and falls. (Allow some moments of silence.)

EMPOWERMENT Bonding With The Ancients

Two women go to the altar and take the bowl of ashes, a candle and the hand mirror. They return to the circle. While one woman holds the candle and the mirror, the other woman begins to paint with ashes the face of a woman in the circle. They chant while all join in:

> **Ancient Mother**
> **I hear you calling**
> **Ancient Mother**
> **I hear your song**
> **Ancient Mother**
> **I hear your laughter**
> **Ancient Mother**
> **I taste your tears.**

(Once again, one drummer leads the beat.)

Each woman's face is painted; the mirror is held up to her and the chant continues. Proceed clockwise around the circle until everyone's face is painted.

The Chant rises and a dance begins with one woman leading the circle around the altar. The circle snakes outward and around the room forming a spiral dance.

End with a cone of power around the mountain by increasing the intensity and speed of the drum beat, voices and rhythm instruments.

GROUNDING

RETURN STONES

OPEN CIRCLE

CELEBRATE

INVOCATION TO PERSEPHONE

Dark Goddess, whose power lies deep in the Earth's heart,
    I hold tightly the memory of your return.
Dark Goddess, whose mountains are the lost temples,
    I move through your narrow passage to find you.
Dark Goddess, whose womb holds the life seed,
    I turn inward to the cave tomb waiting.
Dark Goddess, whose changes reflect a timeless pattern,
    I stand in the realm of your Ancient spiral.
Dark Goddess, whose sorrow sustains life,
    I cradle your tears as my ancient wisdom.

NORTH CHANTS

Ancient Mother[7]

Ancient Mother
I hear you calling
Ancient Mother
I hear your song
Ancient Mother
I hear your laughter
Ancient Mother
I taste your tears.

    Traditional Neo-pagan chant

Goddess Medley

Isis, Astarte, Diana,
Hecate, Demeter,
Kali, Inanna

    Words by Deena Metzger and
    Music by Caitlin Mullin

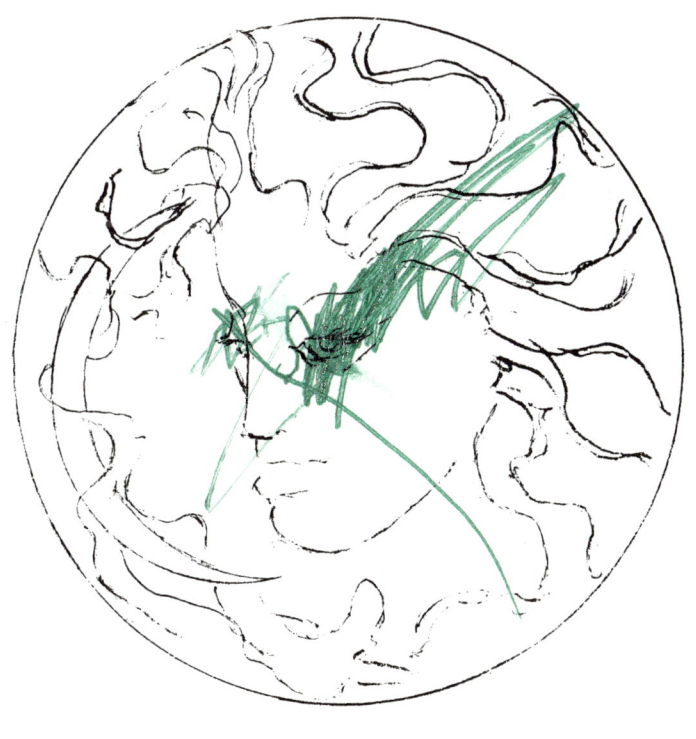

THE EAST

The place of beginnings, dreams and clarity,
The place where visions are born.

INVOCATION

In the East,
> where pale colors of dawn touch sweet scent of lilac,
> I arise.

In the East,
> with long feathery robes,
> my arms open to the universe.

In the East,
> where the sliver of moon rests as a jewel in my heart,
> I wonder.

In the East,
> where the winds become my voice,
> I call.

In the East,
> where I stand with ancient sword in hand,
> I return.

In the East,
> as a gentle warrior,
> I begin.

POWERS OF THE EAST!
BRING YOUR MORNING SONG TO MY HEART,
AND IN RETURN,
I WILL TAKE FLIGHT INTO YOUR DAWN.

FROM THE OLD ONES

The Old Ones teach us that the East is the place of dawn, the ever returning magic of sunrise. The East is the time of spring, when buds break through the dark soil and bring new hope.

In the East, we wait with anticipation for clarity. We learn to define and live our ideals, to take our swords and cut clearly our paths of light through the darkness and the density of our storms.

The East comes to us as the light breaks through the gray hues and turns the world into soft pastel colors. And if we let ourselves become like the bird, soaring high above the clouds, we too will sing.

In the East we call upon the power of our minds to guide us and to clarify our relationship to the Earth and to the universe. We learn new skills on our path. We gain tools that bring us to new perspectives and greater knowledge. We search through our journeys for clues, and we learn to understand our experiences. As dawn lightens the sky, the Mysteries illuminate our minds. Symbols and messages come to us as inspiration.

The wisdom of the East is often demonstrated in fairy tales or myths when the the main character comes to a point in the story where she is exhausted and disillusioned, lost in a maze, a dark forest or a strange land. She has reached the gateway of the East, where she sits, tired and despairing. As she tells her story, she unravels the clues which will lead her out of the maze.

Sometimes enlightenment appears in the form of a bird, a fairy, or an old, wise woman. The seeker receives a gift of the East, an awareness of her magical powers. Believing in this magic, she becomes ready to resume her quest.

We often need to sift through our stories to be able to understand their deeper meanings. When we do, we begin to unlock the Mysteries and touch the thread that we weave through our lives. As we search through our own experiences, we build on the continuum of the ancient myths of all women. Together as midwives we bring the ancient religion of the Goddess alive, carrying her culture outward as tiny sparks of light.

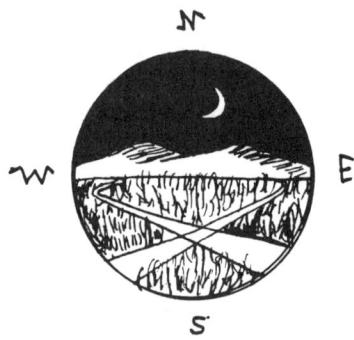

CROSSROADS: MOVEMENT INTO VISION

As I moved into the East, I found myself reevaluating my directions and dreams. Both my intellect and my spirit child were connected to this process.

I decided it was time to look at my skills critically. I needed to challenge myself with new tools to explore the richness of the Mysteries. I wanted to learn about this magic and power I was so drawn to. I studied a variety of divination skills—tarot, astrology and crystals. I studied nature, religion and politics. I studied other people's approaches to ritual and healing. I studied how to move energy and how to wield power. I began to set a new direction for myself and to share the skills I was acquiring as I went down this path.

I also learned to relate to myself and others. I saw my story come alive as I shared in circle. I saw how I had struggled as a child to belong, how I had kept alive the magic through pain and often despair. And as I went over the many upheavals and nightmares, I saw how truly strong I had been as a child. I had survived and my spirit child had kept the secrets of the vision alive.

I discovered, as I stood at the gateway of the East looking at these lessons and challenges, that I valued the romantic, the dreamer, the part of me that will not let go of hope! And that was what I gave rebirth to in the East—my vision. I wrote the story of Little Bird. It was the story of my spirit child. The other stories followed. When I reread the stories a few years later, I saw their connections to my story. They were the thread I weaved on my path toward power.

I have learned that the people I find spiritually powerful believe in the dreams the spirit child weaves from the beginning of time, before time and after time. It is in the East that we open to that vulnerability. It is there the spirit child tells you her story from the beginning of time, before time and after time. When we believe in the dream she weaves, we begin to see the visions through the eyes of the maiden aspect of the triple Goddess. And our healing grows as we bond with other women, sharing our ideals.

I have listened to many women talk about their lives. They shared their pain, their fears, their joy and their power. A common factor was a quest for healing, a determination to reclaim their power. Visions were being created from their pain and confusion.

One day while sitting in circle with a large group of women, I felt a new immanent presence. I felt it as a breathing, living, healing energy with a pulse that bonded the women in the group. I saw it grow as the women gathered in council and spoke their wisdom.

My own vision became clear that day. I saw that we were gathering as women to put the pieces back together in our lives, in our herstory, in our religion and in the world. And from that day on, it became clear to me that piece by piece the Goddess is re-membered. Piece by piece, with her, we too heal into power.

EAST EXERCISE I: BEGINNINGS

Materials: Flower petals, cornmeal or tobacco to make an offering
A bowl of stones if you are inside

Find a secluded, quiet place, preferably outside, where you can sit and be calm. Close your eyes and begin to relax your muscles. Take a deep breath and imagine as you exhale that you are gently blowing your troubles and fears away. Breathe in and out, letting the fresh air cleanse and soothe you. Now, as you feel relaxed and cleansed, begin to feel the harmony of this place. When you feel a part of your surroundings, acknowledge and call in the powers of the Four Directions by gently breathing in and out the energy of each direction. Imagine a circle of healing, protective light surrounding you. This circle will energize and open all your senses.

When you feel in touch with this circle of light, place your hands on the ground and let the light flow through your fingers like root beams flowing through the dark soil. Touch the Earth's heart and draw her powerful, nurturing energy into your body. Breathe in and out, feeling yourself relax and your senses become clearer and clearer. Give thanks to the Earth and slowly come back to the gentle darkness behind your eyes.

Now, with your senses open and clear, stand up and look around you. Pick up the first stone you see. Then listen for the voice of a second stone.

The first stone is your beginning stone. It teaches you about being open to receiving gifts and approaching new ideas and values. The second stone is the East stone. It symbolizes visions and new paths.

Return with both of your stones. Allow their energy to flow into you. Reflect for a few moments on what they communicate to you. Give thanks to the earth for the stones.

EAST EXERCISE II: FACES OF THE ALTAR

Materials: A quiet place
Many stones or objects that will be placed on an altar
Five candles

Go to a quiet place where you can relax and meditate undisturbed. Bring with you a pile of small stones (including your beginning stone from Exercise I) and five candles.

Invite the powers of the Four Directions to be there with you. Starting in the East, welcome the power of clarity, the ability to begin and to dream. In the South, welcome the power of will, the spirit of passion and desire. In the West, welcome the courage to dare to look inward, the power to change, the ability to let go. And in the North, welcome the power to be still, to be silent, to touch ancient wisdom. In your mind draw a circle of light around you. Touch the Earth and give thanks. Go into the silence of this sacred place you have created and be one with its harmony.

Place a candle in the north, east, south and west points of your circle. Keep the fifth candle next to you as you sit in the eastern part of the circle, turning toward the northeast, which will represent your present. Ask yourself,

Where have I been?
What have I sought?
What have I found?
What did I lose?

Ask yourself as many questions as needed to help define your present.

Imagine yourself as the character in a fairy tale who sits in a dark forest or in a labyrinth searching for clues out of the maze. Allow yourself to feel these questions in the depths of your heart. With each question choose a stone that symbolizes the feelings, experiences and answers to the questions. Bring the stone to your heart and then place it on the earth next to the east candle.

When you feel complete with your present, light the candle symbolizing the shedding of light on the questions you have uncovered.

Now turn to the northwest which will represent your past. This may symbolize your childhood or a more recent past. This is the northwest passage, the gate to transformation—letting go, death, rebirth. Turn to the northwest and ask,

What did I end?
What did I change?
What did I feel?
What courage did I find?
What seeds did I plant in the Earth for the passage of winter?
What were my fears?

As always, ask as many questions as necessary to compose a clear picture of your past. With each question, bring a stone to your heart and place it on the north point of your circle next to the candle. Light the candle symbolizing the shedding of light on this passage.

Now turn to the South and take two new stones, one to represent your spirit child and the other your spiritual warrior. Let them touch, bring them to your heart and place them on the Earth in the South.

The South represents your future and involves acting on your power. Imagine yourself finding a way out of the labyrinth you are caught in. Ask yourself,

> *What do I desire?*
> *What do I want?*
> *What is my passion?*

Be with the stones that you have placed in the various points. Take in once again their meaning and connection to you.

Then begin to choose stones one at a time that represent issues that you feel should be addressed. For example, you may feel that your passion is consuming your life and that you are out of control. Maybe your passion needs some wisdom applied to it. If so, take the stone symbolizing passion and place it in the North.

When you are finished, look at the altar you have built to understand your patterns. You have built an altar that tells your story. Our altars become like the lines and expressions on our faces—they tell our stories.

Now light the fifth candle and place it in the East. This candle symbolizes the place of clarity and enlightenment. This is where we invite the magic to enter our lives. Take one more stone, the beginning stone from Exercise I, and bring it to your heart, make a wish, call upon the power of magic. Place it between the South and the East, and let it be the stepping stone to your journey onward.

EAST VISUALIZATION: DAWN

Materials: A candle

Allow yourself to sink deeply into a relaxed, comfortable position. Taking deep breaths, let all remaining tensions slip away. Feel the strong support of the Earth as her rhythmic, nurturing energy flows into your body . . . . Breathe in and out, letting the air cleanse you while you relax your muscles with each breath . . . . Soon the air will do the breathing for you as your body sinks into a deep rest. Your mind will become clearer with each breath of air that pours into you.

As you rest behind the warm darkness of your eyes, imagine having been on a long journey in a place far away in ancient times . . . . It is just before dawn and you are walking down a path that leads to a beautiful clearing. Breathe in this special place, observing all that surrounds you and find a comfortable spot to sit facing East. Allow your senses to become one in harmony with this place . . . .

As you relax and enjoy the tranquility of this place, call your spirit child to your side. Welcome her, give her a gentle hug, and let her settle down next to you facing East. As the two of you watch the sky, you see that the colors have become lighter and that there are only a few faint outlines of wispy clouds . . . . Maybe you can hear a bird in the distance . . . . Breathe in and out, taking in the excitement of the approaching dawn . . . . You have journeyed far and have learned much. Ancient wisdom surrounds you as you rest . . . let your spirit child get up and play. Allow her to dance. Let her explore, let her be in her beauty. Soon she will return with a treasure, a gift for you . . . .

When she comes back, have her sit down once again next to you. Together you see on the horizon the pulsating, brilliant pink glow of the sun as it slowly rises in the sky. Allow this light to flow through you and your child . . . . Breathe in and out, letting every pore of your body soak in this warm, healing energy from the universe . . . . Watch your child as she sees and feels this great beauty . . . . Let her teach you her ways. Allow yourself to become your child . . . . Watch the sunrise the way your child watches . . . Breathe in and out in this boundless joy . . . . See how the whole sky has filled with this pink, pulsating glow. See all of nature as a child sees it, as one with this pulsation. Breathe in and out. Be with this moment . . .

As the sun has reached halfway to its zenith, see how clear and fresh everything around you becomes. Allow this clarity to fill you. Now bring your spirit child into your heart and give thanks to the sun and your surroundings. Slowly touch the Earth, thanking her for her gifts, and when you are ready, follow the path that brought you to this place until you again find yourself behind the warm darkness of your eyes. Tap the earth and return to the place you began this journey.

THE SILVER THREAD III

                THE STORY OF LITTLE BIRD

East had disappeared.
She was gone.
Nowhere to be found.
One night, tired, confused and disillusioned, East gathered her feathery robes of pastel colors and left to search for a quiet place to hide and to rest.
It was in the beginning of time, before time and after time. East, the place of dreams, of beginnings and clarity, was gone, and a deep loss and frenzy spread across the land. All joined together in search of East.

In a dark forest not far away, under a tall oak tree lived Little Bird. She was different from most birds, for she had a broken wing and had been lame for as long as she could remember.

But she seemed to be a happy little bird. She enjoyed her home of sweet moss and fern. She had come to know and love the forest floor. While other birds sang from high branches, she chirped her song next to the massive roots of her oak tree. Earth had come close to protect her from the fierce animals and the frightening storms. Earth had helped her feel special, and in her tiny heart she felt truly loved.

She lived quietly and simply. She spent many hours dreaming, listening to the trees as they sang in the wind. She enjoyed the silent waters of the lake. Sometimes she felt she was the fairy queen who ruled the forest. There she would sit on her moss throne, and the world around her seemed to sparkle with magic.

    Her favorite pastime was to sit and stare up at the sky, seeing the changes through the day. She watched the sun rise in glory. She marveled at the pale colors reflected on the ever-so-slowly-moving clouds that sprawled across the blue air. She dreamed she was there up above the clouds, swirling, soaring and dancing in the warm sunlight.

    When night came, she told the stars about her dreams. And when the moon came to stand next to the stars, she felt a tranquility flow into her heart as she settled into the moss to rest. Sometimes she dreamed the stars came to lift her to the sky, and she flew free in the heavens, a beautiful, dark silhouette against the silvery-blue moon.

During the day her friend Fawn often came and sat down beside her and listened to her stories and dreams about the sky. Sometimes she sang a new song for him that she had learned from one of the trees. She always listened very carefully to the different songs each tree sang as the wind blew through its leaves, and in time she had learned them all. Fawn stared in wonder with his soft brown eyes. He couldn't fully understand Little Bird's joy, for his joy was in running through the woods free and alert. Sitting quietly and gazing up at the sky did not appeal to him. But he listened with great patience to his little friend.

One day Fawn came to her in a great hurry to tell her of East's disappearance. He told her about the frenzy and despair that was spreading across the land and how everyone had joined in the search for East. Little Bird was alarmed by the news but did not understand. Her world seemed the same. Fawn announced he was joining the search and was going to have to leave. Little Bird felt sad, for she would miss Fawn's company, and she wished she could join in. But she was lame and had to stay close to home.

That night Little Bird was a bit sad and lonely. She missed Fawn, and she worried about the despair that was spreading across the land. She did not wait for the moon to rise that night; instead, she snuggled close to the warmth of Earth and fell fast asleep.

As she slept, a firefly came to her. His soft green light flickered until she awoke. She blinked a few times, thinking she was dreaming. But then the firefly spoke: "I am Firefly from the South," he whispered. "I am a messenger of the spirit."

Little Bird did not quite understand what he meant, but she listened carefully. "Follow me to the lake," he said.

Little Bird tilted her head, carefully watching Firefly as he flew from leaf to leaf in the direction of the lake. She knew that at nighttime the lake's water became very still, just like a mirror in which she could see the stars and the moon. There was a beauty about the lake at night that filled Little Bird's heart with wonder.

So she decided to follow Firefly down the path.

    As she arrived, an omniscient presence filled the stillness of the night. Waiting near the lake was Fire, her power sparkling in the dark. This frightened Little Bird, for she had never been so close to the power of Fire before. She began to tremble as Fire spoke: "I am Fire from the South, I speak of will of the spirit. I have sent Firefly to you because his light is like your gentleness." She smiled, saying, "I am glad you chose to follow him here."

    Little Bird listened as Fire's voice began to bellow. "The frenzy is crossing the land. All have gone in search of East. And yet all have failed to find her." Little Bird began to tremble again.

    Earth moved close with her mountains outstretched. Her quiet stillness soothed Little Bird's trembling heart. Little Bird felt so small and insignificant in the presence of such great powers, but she listened carefully.

    "I am Earth, from the North. I gave you my trees, and with joy you listened carefully to their voices and you understood."

With her gentle ripples, Lake then reached out to Little Bird and beckoned her to come close. "I am from the West; I gave you my still waters and you saw the stars." She smiled, saying, *"You looked deep into my waters and dreamed."*

"Now little one, come close and see." Little Bird did so. *She went to the edge of the lake and looked into the waters.*

As she peered over the grass dune, she saw Lake's gentle ripples. Then she saw the sky reflected in the center of the lake, her wonderful sky, with the stars twinkling and the moon setting. Ah, the moon, her friend who came to soothe her at night. She breathed in the heavens and felt their joy.

As she looked at the water, she saw herself, a little bird with a broken wing. As she continued to stare, she saw a light emerge from her breast. It seemed to grow from her heart. It grew and grew and she began to feel the breeze under her wings, a cool, gentle breeze that lifted her high up into the stars. Little Bird realized that she was in the sky. She was her spirit flying free as dawn appeared.

As she soared above the clouds, she heard the voices of the trees, the lake and the sun whispering, "Little Bird, it is in your gentle heart that East has gone to hide, to rest."

It was in the beginning of time, before time and after time. And East had been found.

THE EAST RITUAL: TAKING FLIGHT

INTENTION

This is a ritual to find our visions, dreams and clarity. We create decorative scarfs to symbolize reclaiming our visions and dreams.

MATERIALS NEEDED
   Smudging, sage and shell
   Material—chiffon or transparent cloth,
     large enough to wrap around one's shoulders
   Sparkles and glue
   Candles and candle holders
   Water cauldron or bowl
   A basket of cards with one healing word on it e.g., love, peace,
     truth, freedom, confidence

CHANTS "Magic is Afoot;" "Bird Woman;" "Story Woman."

CLEARING

GROUNDING AND CENTERING

SMUDGING "Bird Woman" can be sung during smudging.

CASTING CIRCLE

INVOCATION To Athena

STORY Story of Little Bird or one of your own.

DRAMATIZATION
Around a cauldron of water in the center of the circle is a rainbow of scarfs and containers of sparkles and glue. One at a time, a woman comes forward to the center, says her name and states, "I am a woman with a vision of (myself, this region and/or the world) . . ." She then shares a brief story about her vision. The group responds by acknowledging her sharing with, "(Name) is a woman who tells us her vision . . ."

   She turns to the cauldron and puts some water on her face or other parts of her body to bless her vision.

She then chooses a "vision scarf." She and the circle chant, "The Goddess is alive, magic is afoot," while she sprinkles sparkles and glue on the scarf, focusing on the future she wishes to bring to her life. The circle responds as she lights a candle in the center.

If a woman does not have a vision or ideal to move toward, she can select a card and speak to the current or potential significance for her of the word that is on the card, and then create a scarf reflecting that word.

EMPOWERMENT
After all have participated, begin a chant and special dance with "A River of Birds in Migration." Raise a cone of power around the cauldron and then ground it as the chant dies.

One woman goes to the center and blows out the candles, saying, "We send the energy of the East into the world on the smoke of these candles." The circle then chants, "We are the story women."

GROUND

RETURN STONES

OPEN CIRCLE

CELEBRATE

INVOCATION TO ATHENA

Athena, strong and beautiful—Ancient Warrior,
   come enwrapped in your winged power.
Call upon your heartsong to open the skies.
Spread rainbow light across sea cliffs.
Cloaked in power, raise the sun, piercing the grey mist at dawn.
Athena, oh great one! who defies time and challenges the form.
Free the words in our story and hold the ideal as our voice.
With the courage of a sacred warrior, offer our hearts as a painted
   vessel to the heavens.

EAST CHANTS

The Goddess is alive,
magic is afoot[8]

      (spoken not sung)

A River of Birds in Migration

A river of birds in migration
a nation of women with wings.

Goddess Medley

We are strong women
We are story women
We are healers
Our souls will never die

      Australian Women's chant
       (adapted by Starhawk)

THE SOUTH

The place of will, passion and desire.
The power to act, to be, to heal.

INVOCATION TO THE SOUTH

I circle 'round and 'round
      spinning a web of fire.
I return to be,
      to feel, to touch, to heal.
I am the fire,
I am the spirit,
I am the child.
From my fingertips I cast forward my light,
with depth of heart I breathe in your love
Alive !
I circle 'round and 'round
      weaving a web of fire.
I am the fire,
I am the spirit,
I am the child.

POWERS OF THE SOUTH,
BRING THE DANCE TO MY BODY.

FROM THE OLD ONES

The Old Ones teach us that in the South we learn to direct our power. We bathe in the light of the full moon and dance in the warmth of the sun. We learn to direct our will, act on our desires and live our dreams.

In the South we experience the power of joy. The vital life force rushes through our bodies, as passionate fires burning into desire.

To the South we bring our inner child to dance and sing. Our spirits grow and bloom into full glory.

In the South we experience our abilities. We wield power, touch the rhythms of our bodies and dare to be all that we envision.

Fire is the symbol of the South. As flames leap upward from the cauldron, radiating warmth outward, we become the fire. Like the sun at midday, we feel the pulsating power of the universe. The continuous beat of the drum joins the rhythm in our hearts; the song tells our stories, and the dance expresses our joy.

In the South we protect our dreams, we rage at the pain; and, like Kali the destroyer, we fight back, hold on and claim what is ours. We create bonds, and we bring back the sacred flame.

Laughter returns, visions become more than an ideal. They lead us, become our reality, the forces behind our actions. We come into our power. We become the dream.

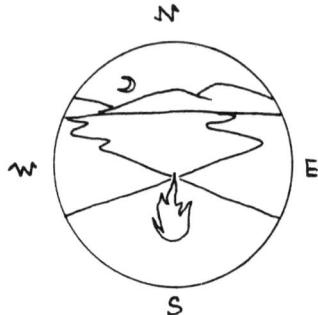

CROSSROADS: MOVEMENT INTO VOICE

As I moved into the last phase of this particular journey, I was once again being challenged to discover a new aspect of my truth.

The Ancients had taken me very deep, and I hadn't been able to escape my own turmoil or my continual sense of emotional vulnerability. I was living on an island, feeling isolated, lost and scared! I needed to ground myself in the woods, where I go for peace and centering. But this island had no woods, only water and more water.

I knew the Ancients had some part in this predicament. In many cultures this kind of situation is referred to as the workings of the trickster or the sacred clown, whose function is to bring upheaval and new ways through tricking us to let go. The Ancients had been calling me ever since I had arrived here, and I had been ignoring their voices.

One day I was standing on a high dock which led into the ocean. An old man in his late seventies and a young boy were fishing. Suddenly, floating by, gasping for air, was a baby wood thrush. I quickly said to the boy and the old man, "We have to do something!"

I don't like swimming, and I hoped the boy would do something, but I knew he really was too young. Both the old man and the boy looked at me dumbfounded. They claimed it was dead or would be dead soon and why bother. I explained that I just couldn't stand there and watch it die without trying to save it.

Both the old man and the young boy were adamant that I should not jump in, but I ignored them and swam to rescue the bird, who had floated farther away on the outgoing tide.

The bird was still alive. I had started to swim back with it when I realized I was hyperventilating from the shock of the cold water. I was gasping for air, I couldn't get my voice, and I didn't see how I was going to pull myself out of the water! I couldn't breathe, I couldn't talk, and I couldn't swim to shore. I was scared and was holding back panic.

As a true intellect and Aquarian, I started to have thousands of philosophical thoughts. I had learned an old survival trick: when you don't have an immediate solution, think about something else. That did help me calm down and float, while I took little breaths. Suddenly I found a stump near the dock post that enabled me to reach high up and find strength I had not had before. I pulled myself out of the water.

Gasping, I held the little bird. It was dying. It looked up at me with glazed eyes. I knew it was time to offer it to the spirits, and to the warm life force of the sun. It died cupped in my hands.

The old man and young boy watched the whole thing in amazement. "You are sure a strange lady," stated the boy. "It was going to die, you know, and you couldn't keep it alive!" His voice sounded angry, as if for a moment he had hoped that there was going to be a miracle. I could feel his disillusionment creep in.

"I told you not to dive in, but no one ever listens to me," accused the old man. In his eyes I could see he had actually been impressed by my actions, though he would not reveal such approval.

I told them I had to dive in. I had to try! The bird died knowing someone had tried to save it.

I realized later that this little bird was a part of the Earth, too little, too wounded to be saved. It was a part of you and a part of me. This experience brought me to a deeper understanding of the power to know when the wheel of fate is turning, the snake is shedding, Hecate is wooing. I also came to see that although the healer must learn that she cannot save it all, she must be vulnerable to that which cannot be saved. And out of this vulnerability, the spiritual warrior can find, somewhere deep in the dark despair of the nightmare, the courage to fight for the dream.

A few nights later, I called a friend who is a channeler, hoping he would give me answers. He replied, "The only message I am receiving is that I am not to give you any answers. You must talk to the Ancients and use your drum."

I lit the candles, prepared the altars and called in the powers. I drummed and drummed until I heard their message. "You have been brought to this island to finish this book," they told me. "You will do nothing else until then! We have isolated you so this may happen. You are here in this place to call alive the spirits in this land. You are here to help create a passage for the return of many Ancients into this time so they may be a part of Earth's healing. Her body, her heart and her spirit are calling out to all healers, past and present.

"From now on in each ritual you do, your drum beat will become a call to the spirits of the land. You will be calling the healers to rise from the earth. No matter where you are, you will call, and we will always be with you. So go drum the heartbeat of the land and teach others to do the same."

As I drummed that night in the candlelight in front of the Goddess statues, I felt the power as I never had before. There was a new rhythm in the sound of my drums, and the room filled with a healing energy.

I began to envision the dream. I chanted over and over again Starhawk's chant:

> Let it begin with every step we take.
> Let it begin with every change we make.
> Let it begin . . . .
> We are the Goddess giving birth to ourselves.
> We are the Goddess giving birth to ourselves.

I felt the spirits around me. I felt the Goddess as if she were time herself! I saw the Goddess. I saw time converge and evolve from within a dark abyss. I saw, in the flicker of a moment, timelessness. I felt myself in the power, and I felt myself as the power. I knew she was showing me how we can all step into our power.

I went out to the porch. I drummed to the land and turned the dream into my Being. As I stared up at the stars, I came to know the Old Way, and in the Old Way I reached out and held the moon.

Now, as I stand in the South, I share with you a poem. It is the living flame that rises from my cauldron. It is for the Old Ones.

CICADA

> Ancient One, Wise one, Old Mother,
> aged woman squatting in the sand,
> like a primordial bird
> hovering and waiting in the stillness.
> The only movement is your feathers shifting
> with the dry wind.
> Warm sand bulges into form,
> outlining copper tones on blue skies.
> The heat is healing your bones as it dries your skin.
> Out of the desert's silence I hear the panting of your
> hot breath, pulsating across time.
> And then I hear many hot breaths.

I see many squatting women in a circle.
The Ancient Ones
breathing life into Earth's body.

And the cicada tells me it is time.

The Ancient Ones, whose glance carries the power of a hawk's
    claw.
The Ancient Ones, whose eyes search mine,
bringing me back.
The Ancient Ones, whose hands reach out
touching my deep longing.

Aged Ones, Old Ones, Wise Mothers,
across time I whisper for you to come.
My laments turn into rhythmic moans,
moving deep within me.

And the cicada tells me it is time.

Across all boundaries and time, I return to you,
Goddesses of our ways.
I taste your sweet fruit warmed by the sun,
soothing my dried throat.
I call to you
uncoiling like the serpent,
rhythms open, stirring inside me.
My deep throated call beckons across the desert
answered by squatting women in open spaces.

And the cicada tells us it is time.

The serpent spirals outward across sound.
Our voice becomes her voice,
her vibrations ripple through us,
turning time into rhythm and rhythm into time.

Spinning, I find myself between the Ancient and the Aged.
Oh, Ancient Mother, Aged One, can you see me as I see you?

Old Woman, your temple lies still in your heart,
but all dear to you lives in me.

And for this moment we will forget the pain,
the stones crumbling from our temples,
the fires burning our bodies,
the raged wars and then the silence.

For this moment we will remember the fire
as our sacred flame in the wells of the temples.
We will remember the dark blue and white mosaic
patterns that swirled as we danced.
We will remember the women hand in hand, moving to the
blue flame that emerged from the darkness of the earth.

And the cicada tells us it is time.

For this moment our serpents uncoil together.
Deep into my spiral I weave into yours,
and within the beat, my body sways, touching yours.
Old One, Wise One,
our palms press
our hearts breathe
our spirits dance our power, knowing the sacred flame
lives.
It is ours inside forever!
Together, we dance the return.
We shapeshift our place, our time.
For one moment across the sands
I become you and you become me
> The Old Ones
> The Wise Ones
> The Ancient Ones.

SOUTH EXERCISE I: MIRRORS

Materials needed: A large mirror

Stand in front of a mirror with your arms opened wide. Breathe in and out relaxing your body. Feel the flow of the Earth's energy come through your feet. Let this energy spiral upward into your heart. Open your hands and imagine pulling down beams of light from the universe. Breathe in and out, developing a rhythmic flow to your breath and within your body. Imagine waves of energy pouring outward toward the mirror.

Now point to your heart in the mirror, saying to your image, "You are The Goddess." Continue to repeat until you feel free and alive. Then smile and say, "I am Goddess." Learn to smile at yourself, learn the joy of being.

Each woman chooses a partner and, facing each other, repeats this exercise.

If you do this as a group, have the mirror apart from the circle. Take turns standing in front of it, as described above. Then, after the partners have finished, form a circle. Each member in turn stands in the South and claims her power as the Goddess. Tell it—sing it—dance it. The circle joins in with drums, applause, howls, songs or whatever feels alive and powerful. End each person's celebration with a "blessed be!" or some other affirmation.

SOUTH EXERCISE II: RAGE

Rage is an energy that can enable us to act. In this exercise, we confront our rage, let it fill our bodies, and, as with all energy, let it be channeled through us. Rage standing still or denied festers, it turns manipulative and destructive. It is vitally important to release and direct it outward in a constructive way.

Stand with legs apart. Center your body by taking a deep breath to release distractions and tension. With your hands outward and down in front of you, pull the fire of rage from the center of the Earth into your arms, onward to your heart and into all of your body. Feel your strength, your power. Raise your hands cupped as if you held a stone over and just behind your head. Feel its weight, its solidness.

With all your force, throw the stone out and away from you. Your hands should end up in front of you, similar to the pose of a diver. Feel the energy flow out and away from the tips of your fingers. See how far the stone, the energy, stretches out in front of you.

Now, image how you wish to direct this energy. Where do you want it to go? What do you want it to do? Continue to throw it toward an envisioned object. Allow the energy to be released and image it as effective.

If your rage is such that you need to let go of it, continue with the next exercise. If not, consider this a separate exercise.

SOUTH EXERCISE III: PALMS UPWARD

Stand with legs apart. Center yourself with deep breaths. Turn your palms upward toward the universe and open your arms wide on either side of your body. Imagine the universe and thousands of twinkling stars. As you draw the energy to the center of your palms, the stars will be pulled down into your hands. Imagine sparkling star dust. When your hands are cupped and full of star dust, sprinkle or pour this gentle, lyrical energy onto the Earth and over you.

Take another deep breath and repeat the exercise. You may just want to continue to pull the twinkling stars down and play with them. Do that for a while and then begin to cast this energy outward. Let your hands cast waves of healing light.

SOUTH EXERCISE IV: CIRCLE ENERGY

This exercise allows you to experience the diversity of energy in a group and ways the group may shape it. Standing in a circle, each person rubs her hands together. The heat and friction in your palms helps open your heart chakra. Do this for a minute or so. Then cast the energy out to the center by opening your palms toward the center of the circle. Feel the tingling as the energy flows out of your hands.

When you feel it stop, shake your hands, break the connection and release the last bit of energy.

Take a deep breath and draw inward the circles of energy to fill your body. Soon your body will feel a tingling, lighter sense about it.

One woman stands and goes to the center of the circle. She picks up the energy there between her hands or arms and carries it over to the woman on her left. The woman on her left accepts the energy and passes it on clockwise. Allow the energy to go around and around the circle building power, changing shape, size and texture.

Watch what happens to the energy and the people. Allow the energy to go around the circle several times. Give each woman a chance to feel the differences in energy forms. When it seems appropriate, release the energy upward to the universe or down to the earth.

Note: you may wish to continue to experiment with all these forms of energy. If these are group exercises, you may also wish to share insights about when each is appropriate.

SOUTH VISUALIZATION: BETWEEN THE FLAMES

Take a deep breath, allowing every particle of your body to dissolve and blend with the warm darkness of the Earth. . . . As you rest with the darkness, your energy flows and merges with the pulsation of the Earth's heart. . . . Hear the beat, over and over again. . . . This sound fills your body as a warm, throbbing energy. . . . Take another deep breath. . . . A warmth begins to tingle through you, starting at your toes . . . up to your legs . . . into your belly. . . . Let it fill your lungs and move down your arms, tingling into your fingertips. . . .

Breathe deep and let it move up your spine, up your neck, and to your face, flowing onward to the top of your head. Feel its force moving through you. . . . See the energy as it spirals around you. . . .

Deep in the core of this warmth, a cave entrance appears. . . . You can feel and hear a pulsating sound coming from a light inside the cave. . . . Breathe deep into your belly and walk through this tunnel toward the light. . . . Hear the sound. . . . Feel the pull as it draws you inward. . . . The light touches you and blends with your center. . . . Breathe in and out. . . .

As you move through the cave, notice the walls . . . the ancient markings. Look at the shapes and colors. . . . Feel the energy vibrating from the images. . . . The cave becomes the Earth's womb, alive and breathing. . . . Breathe in the energy of the Earth. . . . Feel the pulsation. . . .

Follow the light until you have arrived at an opening. . . . You look in through this opening and see that the light has been coming from a beautiful fire burning in the center of an ancient stone circle . . . . Go to the fire. . . . The flames leap and dance in front of you. . . .

The flames lure you, drawing you closer. . . . Take time to be with this sacred fire. . . . Feel its power as you breathe in the nurturing warmth. . . . This is a place of power and you are to remember your power. . . . This is your sacred place, and it is where you go to be healed. . . .

You are here to remember the ancient flame. . . .

the ancient flame that calls—to burn—to become—to return . . .

You stare deep into the fire and remember a time long ago when you stood drawing energy from a great cauldron.... Inside the cauldron, swirling, moving, pulling, was unleashed power.... Like an ancient serpent, wild and spiraling, the power calls you.... Breathe in the power.... Your breath becomes the breath of the serpent.... See how she hisses and spits orange flames.... She leaps outward, shimmering, and then spirals downward, diving into the sacred flame....

Breathe in and out.... You are dissolving with each breath into a magnetic flow of energy.... Open your arms and welcome this sensuous power into your body.... Watch the flames change color .... Raise your hands, pulling the flames higher.... Connect with the power ... sway with the flame ... become the fire.... Breathe in the energy....

You are here to remember the ancient flame ...

the ancient fire that calls—to burn—to become—to return ...

You continue to stare deep into the fire. You remember another time, long ago in the dark times, when the flames carried pain.... You are here to remember that pain and the sorrow and to heal them. You are here to remember the cries and to feel the rage of the oppressed, the burned ... the rage and pain of the women who died as Witches. These women have called you here to remember their sacred flame. In the movements of the flame, as they burned, each one released her power to the flame for safekeeping.... See the power as it burns in the flame.... Listen to the Ancients calling you....

Listen to the heart of the great fire.... In this heart you will find the great spirit—alive—returned from those who burned.... It is the ancient flames that you call back into your heart as you remember the fires of the dark times.... The flames call out, saying "No more shall we burn in pain!".... Stare deep into this burning power.... The flames whisper to you, saying "No more do we burn in despair ... no more".... The truth hides in the core, and you have returned to reclaim this truth.... Breathe in the energy....

You are here to remember the ancient flame....

the ancient fire that calls—to burn—to become—to return....

Deep in the very core of these flames you come to the present time of the burning flames . . . . Their beauty dances in front of you . . . . Breathe in this beauty . . . . Move deep into the power . . . deep into the rhythmic flow . . . deep into the pulsating heat . . . deeper and deeper into your own sacred space . . . . The warmth of the fire spirals upward inside you . . . . In these flames you see the colors as they move and change . . . .

An image of the Goddess begins to appear . . . . Move closer into the flames . . . . Feel her truth flowing into you . . . . Look into her eyes . . . touch her . . . rest with her . . . . Breathe deep into her body . . . . Let her breath become your breath, her heartbeat become your heartbeat . . . . Breathe deep into her power, her warmth, her rhythm . . . . Feel her body as she begins to intertwine with yours, like a vine growing through you and into you . . . .

Feel her life force, as roots, burrow deep inside . . . . Your body receives her . . . . Her flames form and change, burning warmly . . . . Her energy pours into you . . . . Open your soul to her power . . . . Breathe in and out, becoming one with her sacred flame . . . .

You are here to remember the ancient flame . . . .

the ancient fire that calls—to burn—to become—to return . . .

Soon it will be time for you to leave this fire. As you rest, feel the calmness in the flames. Feel the healing energy and the power . . . .

It is time now to move out of the fire and back into the sacred stone circle . . . . Touch the Earth and return to the cave entrance . . . .

When you are ready, move through the cave back to the warm darkness behind your eyes. Give thanks to the Ancient Ones and open your eyes.

SPIRALING OUTWARD INTO POWER FROM THE OLD ONES

It is in the power that we activate what we desire, what we dreamt in the East. We make our act of power, that is we turn our energy outward to the Earth and to others. We build our dreams, hold onto our hopes, and our desires are no longer a fantasy but rather become a concrete reality that we can see happening. Like the warrior's staff, we hold onto this powerful force. It becomes our hands reaching out, touching each other. It becomes the book written, the poem shared, the voice in the song, the drum beat, the standing as resistance for the earth, holding the dying and welcoming the unknown.

In the power we can be the birth-givers, the protectors. In the power we also may be called upon to aid death so as to save the small from pain. It is in the power we are asked to move through our fear and into our voice as we claim the word witch and know we are alive.

Come stand in the center; stand strong and powerful. Become your dream, reach out, touch and be touched. As your feet stand firm on the ground and you feel the fiery energy radiating upwards, become a gentle warrior spirited by the stars before you. And, with the ancient power of all women, raise your hand, touch the heavens and take the moon in hand. And in doing so, come to know that we have lived the flames and we have survived. And it is we who stand in the power, and we are the Ancient ones who return.

BLESSED BE.

THE SILVER THREAD IV

THE STORY OF RABBIT

In the South,
  In the beginning of time, before time and after time,
  Fire lay silent,
  her spirit had been broken.

  Her great flames that once leapt upward lay still and quiet, leaving only a few smoldering embers in the dense fog. Her will to endure had been engulfed by this fog of pain. A chill had spread across the land. Trees that once had swayed in the summer breeze stood still, and brooks that once gurgled joyfully remained silent.

In the West, Sea's great waves rose and became awesome, foreboding and cold.
In the East, summer winds turned into fierce storms that darkened her gentle skies.
The Earth in the North came close and held Fire in her arms, bringing the few remaining embers to her heart.
But the chill continued to spread silently across the land.

    One day Rabbit, the most timid of animals, peered out of her dark hole in the forest. She hopped over to the edge of the meadow, cautiously sniffed the air and wondered what had changed. A sense of sadness reached her nostrils. An unfamiliar silence surrounded her. Not understanding, she decided to go ask River. River who had flowed so far, surely knew. But Rabbit found River frozen and still!
    "Oh River, what has happened? Speak to me, speak to me!" cried Rabbit.
    A tiny voice came from River saying, "Little friend, follow me. Follow my frozen path to the West."
    Now, Rabbit was a timid creature and did not like to stray far from her home. The thought of leaving her meadow and following River's path frightened her.

But River's voice pleaded and touched Rabbit's heart. Gathering all her courage, she leapt onto River's back and followed the icy path to the West.

It was nighttime when Rabbit finally arrived at Sea's great shore in the West. The misty salt air dampened her fur, and the bitter cold wind burned her ears. She stood alone in the dark. One tiny Rabbit faced Sea's fierce waves as they crashed and clamored against the silvery sands.

"You are a brave little Rabbit to travel so far!" Sea's voice bellowed above the waves.

Rabbit stood very still, her heart trembling with fear as she spoke: "Oh Sea, I am only a little Rabbit, and River sent me to tell you my story." She told Sea how worried and confused she was. She spoke of her long, frightening journey to powerful Sea.

Sea listened carefully to Rabbit's story, her waves calming to a rhythmic roll.

In time she commented, "Yes, little one, there is despair across the land. Fire's spirit has been broken, and a fog has engulfed her will. Earth holds Fire in her arms, protecting her and her few remaining embers."

As Rabbit listened to Sea, she felt sadness grow inside her. She stood shivering, her fur wet and cold, silhouetted in the moonlight.

"Little brave one, your journey will be long," said Sea. "The courage that brought you here will stay close to your heart. It is my gift to you."

Rabbit blinked with surprise at such a powerful gift. She thanked Sea.

"Now go find Earth in the North," Sea instructed. "Let her guide you on your journey."

 Rabbit turned away toward the midnight sky and headed North, toward the home of Earth, the place of wisdom and deep silence. In the North, Night spread her starry cloak over the treetops. The land was dark and still except for an occasional howl of a wolf in the moonlight. Dark branches made strange shapes across the forest floor. When Rabbit felt alone and lost, she breathed deeply, and found in her heart Sea's gift of courage.
 She called into the dark for Earth, "Earth, oh Earth, Sea has sent me to you."
 Earth listened. "The land is in despair," Rabbit continued. "Please bring the flames back to Fire's spirit."

Touched by Rabbit's plea, Earth moved closer, wrapping her moonlit mountains around the little creature. "Dear Rabbit," Earth said. "My power is to hold and protect, to nurture and give strength. But I cannot bring the flames back to Fire's spirit."

Rabbit was tired and confused. Her pain grew as she heard Earth's words. Her body ached from the journey, and she was disillusioned. She hovered close to Earth's heart, where the smell of sweet fern soothed her. She burrowed deep into the bed of moss and fell into a quiet sleep. And as she dreamed in the still of the night, she felt Fire's warm embers in Earth's heart. As she slept, a passion grew inside her. An energy she had never known before flowed through her tiny heart. When she awoke, she knew that she had to go in search of the power to restore Fire's flames. "I will go seek the power to heal Fire's spirit!" she exclaimed.

Earth smiled gently and from her highest mountain, she took two small stones. "Here, little one," she said to Rabbit. "Take these stones and hold them close to you, for they hold the power of the North. They will bring strength and wisdom into your heart."

"Now go to the East, my little strong one, to the East where dreams begin and clarity is found."

So Rabbit traveled onward through the night toward the East. Night seemed to endure forever. She felt she was in a long tunnel of darkness. Her only comfort was the familiar scent of pine needles and the occasional flicker of a firefly. In the darkness, Rabbit again became overwhelmed and discouraged, but she held on tightly to Earth's gifts, and the stones gave her the strength she needed.

    Then a wind began to howl through the forest. It was very strong, and it pushed Rabbit forward into the dark, calling, "Follow me, follow me to the cliff, little one."
    As Rabbit followed, she came to a cliff that looked out over the land to the distant mountains. There, standing on the cliff, blowing, whirling, wooing, was Wind.
    Now Rabbit stood strong, held her stones, faced the Wind and waited for him to speak.
    "Place your stones on the cliff," Wind commanded.
    A fear shot through Rabbit. "My stones! These keep me strong, they are a gift from Earth. Surely, if I let them go, you will blow me away! I cannot let go of my stones." She trembled, wondering what Wind would do. She waited, holding them tighter than before.

"Let go of your stones. Place them on the cliff," said Wind. Little Rabbit remained silent.

"Little strong one, search your heart for the gift of the West," Wind instructed. Rabbit did so, and as she remembered the gift of courage running deep, a calmness grew inside her. "Little Rabbit, remember the passion of your journey." Rabbit remembered the warmth that had filled her body as she slept close to Earth's heart. She remembered her journey to find the power to heal Fire's spirit, she remembered why she had traveled so far, so long. And in the depths of her heart, she found courage.

Carefully she placed her two stones on the edge of the cliff. Wind then calmed down to a breeze. Rabbit stood still and waited.

    Time passed and Night began to lift. A soft gray hue surrounded her. A lone bird began to chirp in a nearby tree. The sky turned from a dark pastel blue to a warm violet, dashed with wisps of pink and orange. The air began slowly to warm her body. From behind the mountain, the brilliant red sun rose majestic and powerful. Little Rabbit's eyes filled with tears of joy. This she knew must be where Fire's spirit came from! There in front of her stood a powerful gentle beauty.

    "I am Dawn, Keeper of the East," said Dawn smiling warmly. "I speak of beginnings, of dreams. Dear Rabbit, little dreamer, yours has been a great gift. You listened courageously with your heart and gave your stones. Now I give them back with a new power. They hold the power of dreams.

When you touch them together, they will fill you with Fire's spirit. Now journey to the South."

Rabbit's soft brown eyes twinkled in response. She turned toward the South, the home of spirit, the place of will, passion and desire.

In the South, a quiet stillness and a scent of ashes where honeysuckle had once been, surrounded Rabbit as she came close to where Fire waited. Fire's spirit had been broken, her will to endure lay still. All was very quiet.

Rabbit stood in front of Fire, all alone and yet not scared. "I am Rabbit, and I have a gift for you."

Fire did not respond. She seemed far away, lost in her own despair.

Rabbit thought of her long journey and of what she had found—the tingling energy from the North, the visions in the East and the courage from the West.

She gathered as much power as a little Rabbit could conjure up and exclaimed, "I am Rabbit, and I bring the gifts of the East! I have seen the beauty of your beginnings. I have seen the gift of your spirit!"
Fire listened.

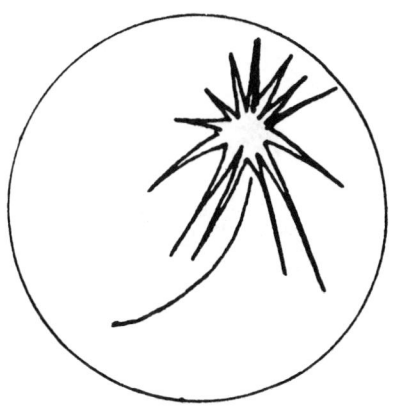

Then Rabbit came very close and pulled out her two stones. She brought them together to touch.
A spark flew up into the sky.
When the spark settled in Fire's heart, a tiny flame began to grow.

    Fire smiled warmly at little Rabbit, and she felt love begin to flow through her again. "Rabbit, my dear one," she said, "You have traveled courageously and far to bring my spirit back. In return, my gift to you from the South will be your new name. Little Rabbit, from now on you will be known as the 'Spirit Keeper.' "

THE SOUTH RITUAL: VOICES IN THE FIRE

INTENTION

This is a ritual in which we find our passion and our power.

MATERIALS NEEDED

    Smudge, sage and shell
    Water
    Small sticks and paper or alcohol and epsom salts to build a fire in the cauldron (for cauldron fire: 2/3 rubbing alcohol, 1/3 epsom salts)
    Stones—one brought by each woman to give away

CHANTS "Air Frees Me," "She Changes Everything," "Dear Friends"

CLEARING

GROUNDING AND CENTERING

SMUDGING

CASTING CIRCLE

INVOCATION To Bridgit

DRAMATIZATION

All chant softly
> *Air frees me*
> *Fire transforms me*
> *Water soothes*
> *Earth heals me*
> *And the balance of the wheel*
> *Goes round and round*
> *And the balance of the wheel goes round.*

    Two women from opposite sides of the circle come to the cauldron. They kneel and face each other, touch stones and tell what power or passion they need. They place the stones in the cauldron and return to the circle chanting. Two other women take their turn. After all have placed their stones in the cauldron, the chant builds as women circle it, drumming and dancing until the energy falls. Allow some silence.

EMPOWERMENT Three women build a fire in the cauldron from paper, sticks and herbs. The women in the circle begin a rhythm by clapping or tapping a beat with their palms on the floor. As the fire builds, they yell out what power is needed. The rhythm builds along with the fire. When all have yelled out what they need, begin to chant:
> *She changes every thing she touches*
> *And every thing she touches changes.*
> *Change is, touch is*
> *Touch is, change is.*

Let the energy build with drumming and dancing until the chant changes into:
> *We are the changers*
> *Every thing we touch changes.*

Allow the energy to rise and fall.
After the fire goes out, the two women who began the ritual go to the center, pour water on the stones to cool them off and chant:
> *Dear friends, dear friends*
> *Let me tell you how I feel*
> *You have given me such treasures*
> *I love you so.*

In pairs, each woman chooses a new stone for the other as her gift of power from the fire. Each says, "This is the sacred stone from Bridget's flame. This stone holds the power to act, to be, to will. Blessed Be."

GROUND

RETURN STONES

OPEN CIRCLE

CELEBRATE

INVOCATION TO BRIDGET

Deep in the well of your darkness your flame burns,
   waiting to be freed as a fire unfolding into power.
The blue flame licks the sacred opening of your temple's well,
   while your priestesses wait for the word to inspire the dance.
Ancient drums pulse deep into our beings the memories of
   our nights where we formed a burning sorrow into the
   strength of an iron gate
   where only the sacred may pass.
Oh Bridget, Goddess of the flame, burn deep
   into the well of my being

SOUTH CHANTS

Air Frees Me

Air frees me
Fire transforms me
Water soothes me (originally water moves me)
Earth heals me
And the balance of the wheel goes round and round
And the balance of the wheel goes round.

traditional Neo-Pagan chant

Kore Chant

She changes every thing she touches
And every thing she touches changes.

We are the changers,
Every thing we touch changes.

Starhawk

Dear Friends

Dear friends, dear friends
Let me tell you how I feel
You have given me such treasures
I love you so.

traditional chant[9]

APPENDIX AND RITUAL TECHNIQUES

APPENDIX

RITUAL

Ritual unlocks the passage to the Mysteries, the realm of the spirit. We enter a passage across time and reality and come to understand "that which cannot be spoken." We bring the Mysteries into our hearts, and we become the weavers of the web of life. We open to the rhythms of nature, Ancient Wisdom and mythologies, and to the stories of women through time and space. We learn the depths of our power, experience our differences and universality, and come to know ourselves.

As we participate in ritual, energy flows and ebbs. Through the movement of our bodies, the challenge of our intellects, the rhythm of our drums, the sharing and the singing, our spirits move—spiraling inward, touching the heart of the universe; spiraling outward—touching one another and the future; spiraling around and around. The swirling energy sends healing power streaming out to others and back to ourselves. It creates patterns that clarify and center us.

As the energy flows around a group, we learn to work together and take risks. It is at the moments when we experience the group as a living organism, pulsing, alive and powerful, leading the way, that we stretch our boundaries, dare to touch our truths, open ourselves to our power and act on our passion.

Ritual is most effective when its structure reflects and helps to allow this flow of energy. The rituals in this book follow such a structure. Each of the elements of that structure is described below.

It is further empowering to know that many different women are coming together in small and large groups all over the world, creating rituals directed toward change, healing and rebirthing. Together, we become the changers who in turn change, we become the healers who in turn heal, we become many who in turn become one!

I invite you to come stand with your feet firmly on the ground, open your arms, raise your outstretched hands to the universe and call upon the power of all women. In doing so you become the changer—and the changed.

SUGGESTED RITUAL STRUCTURE

The rituals and techniques described in this book are suggestions. They are presented in a structure that I have found useful in large groups. It helps me keep a focus on my intentions as I create a ritual.

The structure can be changed and adapted for your needs. Below is an outline, with each part described on the pages that follow.

1. *Clearing*
2. *Grounding and Centering*
3. *Smudging*
4. *Casting Circle*
5. *Invocation*
6. *Story*
7. *Chants*
8. *Dramatization*
9. *Empowerment*
10. *Grounding*
11. *Opening Circle*
12. *Celebration*

In the book, each ritual is preceded by a list of materials needed for the ritual. Prepare or gather these ahead of time and, if appropriate, ask the group to bring items for the ritual.

CLEARING

This exercise is to remove tense and static energy, and help the body to relax and feel refreshed.

Stand with your feet apart. Center your body's weight by swaying back and forth until you feel a grounded space between your legs. Let your arms, shoulders, neck and the rest of your body go limp. Take a deep breath, hold it, then exhale.

Now think of all the tension you have brought to that moment. Allow this tension you feel inside to fill your body as you tense your muscles and hold your breath. Then release and exhale.

Stand with your hands down and in front of you. Slowly, as you breathe deeply, draw energy up from the Earth to your heart with your hands. This is the Earth's powerful healing energy; allow it to flow through your heart and revitalize your center; let it expel what is blocking you. With your hands, push out in front of you as if there were a large object in your way. Allow your breath to push out, letting all the air empty from your belly. Let your hands part and sweep away to either side as if you were swimming the breast stroke.

Begin to build a rhythmic flow by repeating these movements:

UP, OUT and AWAY ...
UP, OUT and AWAY ...

Continue until you feel cleared and relaxed. Then for a few moments, just repeat the "away" or sweeping motion with one hand at a time. Feel the air moving around you.

To finish, bring one more bit of energy up from the Earth, to and through your heart. This time, with palms up and open, let the energy roll down your arms toward the center of the circle. This is cleared, loving energy from your heart and from the Earth's, offered to the center.

GROUNDING AND CENTERING

Grounding is used at the beginning and end of rituals. At the opening of a ritual, you draw energy from the Earth. Return unneeded energy at the end of each ritual as you thank Earth for her gift. As in clearing, we draw energy from the Earth's core.

When we pull energy from the Earth, the objective is to connect with the rhythmic flow of Earth's heartbeat.

In all grounding and centering exercises, we use our body as a vessel through which to channel energy. Energy, like water, follows the path of least resistance, so it is important to relax and open ourselves to its flow.

GROUNDING EXAMPLE: THE TREE OF LIFE

Sit comfortably, leaving your body open to receive energy. Breathe deeply into your belly, feeling the clean, clear air fill your body. Slowly exhale. Repeat this slow, rhythmic breathing—in and out, in and out—throughout the exercise.

Breathe and let your body flow in synchronized rhythm. Place your hands on the ground. Feel them pulsating in rhythm with your breathing. Feel the solidity of the Earth below you and allow your body to rest and settle into the moist dark soil, the warm inviting darkness. As your hands begin to relax, push with your hands as if boring through the soil. Imagine strong roots spreading and flowing from your fingers down into the dark, warm earth.

Picture these roots growing downward and outward, searching for the center of Earth's fire, for the rhythmic vibration of Earth's heart. See the tips of the roots become fine and far-reaching as they work their way around tiny pebbles through the warm darkness. Sense the roots growing from all parts of you as they grow through the ground, searching, longing for the warmth and richness of soil.

When you feel Earth's energy and heartbeat, allow yourself to mingle and be one with this warm, soothing flow. Then begin to pull this power into your roots, feel it flow upward toward you, let it fill every root, spiraling up into your body, your feet, your legs, your belly, your chest, into your arms, your heart, up your spine, your head, and out through your crown chakra at the top of your head. Feel this energy, see if it tingles or is vibrant, whether it warms you or refreshes you. Let it continue to flow up through you.

As you are sending this energy upward, see a magnificent tree trunk growing from you with out-stretched branches reaching up to the sky. See each bud as it blooms and breathes in the air and the energy of the universe. Breathe this energy into your leaves, breathe it down into your branches and down into your roots and down into the dark moistness of the soil to the center of Earth's heart. See how you become the bridge between the universe and the Earth. Breath in, breath out, tingling with each breath.

When you feel vibrant and alive, take the hands of those next to you, gently pushing the energy out through your left hand. Let it pour into the hand of the person on your left. Then gently pull the energy from the person on your right. Continue pushing out, pulling in, as the energy flows in a continuous circuit clockwise. Feel your energy mingling with that of others in the circle as your hands act as transmitters. Breathe in the group's energy. Then place your hands, palms upward, toward the center of the circle, allowing the energy to roll down your arms and out your hands.

When you feel completely relaxed, breathe in the aura from the center of the circle. Take this new energy into your body. See the light that glows from the center. Thank the Earth for her gift.

SMUDGING

Smudging originated as a purification technique, a means of clearing the air. I use smudging as a way to welcome the spirit child to a ritual. I also use it to open our physical sense of smell, to relax our bodies and to affirm ourselves.

I prefer to use a blend of sage, lavender and sweet fern. I find this combination both powerful and soothing. Many people use sweetgrass, juniper, cedar and other herbs and plants. Explore and choose what you find meaningful to you.

Select a shell in which to burn the herb. The shell symbolizes the West, the herbs or plants symbolize the North, the smoke symbolizes the East, and the fire we use to burn the herb symbolizes the South. Thus, the Four Directions are contained in smudging.

Light the herbs. Once a sufficient amount of embers are smoking, raise the shell as an offering to the Four Directions, starting in the East and turning clockwise. Then feel a wish, feel through your body the desire for that wish, allow it to fill your body. With cupped hands, bring the smoke to your heart, where wishes begin and over your head, touching your aura. As you bring the smoke to your heart, feel that the wish has come true and imagine how that feels as a reality.

If two people are smudging, each can hold the shell for the other. If a large group is involved, one person can carry the shell around the circle clockwise or it may be passed around. As it is passed from person to person, it is important to keep the embers lit. When all have smudged, thank the Four Directions and place the shell on the altar in the East, the place of dreams and wishes.

CASTING A CIRCLE WITH STONES

Find a stone for each direction whose energy connects with yours. The stones are a channel through which you can call the powers of the Four Directions. Remember that your body is directly receiving this energy, so it is important to center yourself and to allow energy to flow through you, not into you. The Directions are very powerful, and their energy needs to flow. Imagine light surging through the stone to your hands and up your arms, through your heart and down to the ground. Your body is like a lightning rod. As you practice, you will begin to recognize the uniqueness of each direction's energy as it flows through you.

Stand with your legs apart, feel comfortable, center yourself. Face each direction in turn, starting in the East. Bring that direction's stone to your heart cupped in your palms and feel the stone's energy. Describe the direction in words that are right for you. For example, in describing the North, you might say: "The North, the place of Silence, the power to be still, the place of wisdom, midnight, mountains, dark forest, the wolf."

When you are ready and can sense the power from both your center and from the stones, raise the stone to its direction as you intone: (optional)
>EEEEEEEE for East
>AHHHHHHH for South
>OHHHHHHH for West
>OOOOOOOO for North

All others in the circle should center their bodies and join in calling the Four Directions with you as they raise their arms or assume a similar position. When you feel full and complete, bring the stone back to your heart saying: "I bring the powers to my heart and place the stone on the Earth." Then place the stone on the outside of the circle and repeat the process until all four stones are in place. Thank the powers of the Four Directions and proceed with the ritual.

To return the stones, start in the East and raise the stone to that direction, saying: "I thank the powers of [the direction]. I bring the powers to my heart and place them on the Earth." Each stone is brought back to the center of the circle in this manner.

CASTING A CIRCLE WITHOUT STONES

There are many ways to cast a circle. The use of stones is not necessary. I love stones and choose to use them, but hands alone are perfectly able to pull in energy. Open and raise your arms as you turn to each of the Four Directions, inviting the powers to come.

There are many other ways also. Imagine a light going around the outer circle. This may be a white light or any color you want. Sometimes a circle is cast by walking and sprinkling water on the participants to represent the West, then passing a special stone for the North, feathers for the East and a candle for the South.

Often I will use body movements or sounds for each direction. Further, the circle can be cast by one person, a whole group at once or by four women calling in the Four Directions. The intention in casting a circle is to bring the energy into the circle and have it spiral around, creating sacred space.

INVOCATION

The invocation is also part of casting the circle. It invites the presence of Goddess and/or other energies you wish to work with. It can be a song, a poem or a prose statement. Even a simple gesture—e.g., offering a flower, a sea shell or sharing a piece of art—can serve as an invocation.

The invocation sets the stage for a ritual. It gives the participants an idea of the type of energy they will be working with. It helps us to contemplate our intentions, order our thoughts and connect with our spirits.

CHARGE OF THE GODDESS[10]

I who am the beauty of the green earth and the white moon among the stars and the mysteries of the waters,
I call upon your soul to arise and come to me.
For I am the soul of nature that gives life to the universe.
From Me all things proceed and unto Me they must return.
Let My worship be in the heart that rejoices, for behold all acts of love and pleasure are My rituals.
Let there be beauty and strength, power and compassion, honor and humility, mirth and reverence within you.
And you who seek to know Me, know that your seeking and yearning will avail you not, unless you know the mystery:
For if that which you seek, you find not within yourself, you will never find it without.
For behold, I have been with you from the beginning, and I am that which is attained at the end of desire.

THE STORY

For centuries the art of story telling has been an important element in preserving a culture or a religion. You can use a story, myth or a tale relative to the theme of the ritual. The story can be your own or one you wish to share from another person. As women, we are creating new myths based on our experiences, our herstory and our visions.

In the circle each woman tells her story or one woman is chosen to tell a story. Stories help to weave energy together and bring clarity to the intentions of the ritual.

Another option is a story trance in which one woman tells a story accompanied by a drumbeat, bringing participants into a deep level of the subconscious and creating a space for enlightment to occur.

CHANTS

Chants serve many purposes in a ritual. The words can reinforce the images and intention of the ritual. With their simple and clear lines, they can lead people to act on that intention. Through repetition and sound, energy builds and power is shaped. Finally, chants can help move a circle into places of power.

DRAMATIZATION

Dramatization is the action symbolically portraying the purpose of the ritual. It may be as simple as lighting a candle to symbolize bringing light into your life. It may be much more intricate, such as weaving a web with yarn to symbolize building connections. A dramatization helps the participants explore their purpose and sets in motion energy patterns that are able to change one's life and, ultimately, the world.

EMPOWERMENT

Empowerment literally means the effect of the energy created through the ritual. The time of empowerment in a ritual serves as a way to channel energy toward a cause.

RETURNING THE STONES

To return the stones, one starts in the East, raising the stone to that direction, saying "I thank the powers of [the direction]. I bring the powers to my heart and place them on the Earth." Each stone is brought back to the center of the circle in this manner.

GROUNDING AT THE END OF A RITUAL

To ground at the end of a ritual, place your hands on the Earth to allow unneeded energy to roll down your arms and out your hands back into the Earth. Breathe rhythmically as you release the energy until you feel relaxed, comfortable, rejuvenated but not overcharged. Feel the healing qualities of this energy as it passes through you to the Earth. Exhale and relax.

OPENING THE CIRCLE

We cast a circle when we place stones, call in the Four Directions and invoke the Goddess. At the end of the ritual we release the energy and thank the powers. We establish that we have shifted back into the present. There is also a traditional opening which may be said as the group joins hands:

By the Earth that is her body
By the Air that is her breath
By the Fire of her bright spirit
And the Waters of her living womb
The circle is open but unbroken
May the peace of the Goddess go in our hearts
Merry meet and merry part
And merry meet again.
Blessed Be.[11]

After this a kiss may be passed around the circle, going clockwise. When the kiss has come all the way around and the group is still holding hands, raise them to the sky as a gesture of power and success and then bring them down to the earth.

CELEBRATION

It is fun to have some refreshments after a ritual for grounding and socializing. Ritual is hard work and many people become hungry afterward. It is also a very good time for networking.

THE OFFERING

I dreamt the other night I stood alone in a moonlit field. I was surrounded by shimmering wheat. As I stood there, I saw rising from the earth a dark and Ancient Mother. She towered over me strong and powerful. Like an aged bird she stared silently across the open space. I watched her quietly until she knelt down beside me and gently lifted me into her arms. I lay inside her heart. As I rested in her safe warmth, a rhythmic beat began to vibrate between our hearts. It carried the sound of the river's current and pulled like the force of the tides. It was in the core of the universe and in every blade, seed and tree.

As the pulse grew louder, a momentum of spiraling energy began resounding across the field. She turned toward the mountains in the distance and slowly moved, massive and strong, across the land. Her call was a high-pitched shrill, like some primordial beast. She was the Great Mother in her power, and she was now bringing her children home through a narrow passage.

We are all called to journey through, and become part of, a passage to the hidden place, where the pulse vibrates alive and forever. I realized that when we speak our truths, the passage opens and becomes available to us. It is through our books, our songs, our art, our stories, our actions, our circles and our ancient memories that the Goddess comes, calling us all to heal.

Together again, as the Ancient Ones, we will raise her temple, join in circles and dance the flame. We will be as we are now, an ancient beauty unfolding into time.

With hope, I place this book on her altar.

Blessed be

Eclipse

NOTES

1) The water exercises were inspired by Twylah Nitsch's description of Going Into The Silence in *Indian Medicine Power* by Brad Steiger (Gloucester, MA: Para Research, Inc., 1984), p. 109. Twylah's words in this chapter continue to be a very powerful passage of wisdom for me, and I thank her.

2) The Story of Sea was inspired by a description of a dream in Hyemeyohsts Storm's *Song of Heyahkah* (New York: Ballantine Books, 1972). I wish to thank Hyemeyohsts for his visions and for the true inspiration his writing has had on my work.

3) The chants used in this book, except where otherwise noted, can be found on the Reclaiming Collective's audio-cassette tape, *Reclaiming Chants* (San Francisco: Reclaiming).

4) The Hecate chant, written by Sparky T. Rabbit, was adopted by Starhawk. Other Sparky T. Rabbit chants can be found on the audio cassette tape *Lunacy*, available from Sparky T. Rabbit, P.O. Box 10491, Kansas City, MO 64111.

5) "We All Come From the Goddess" has been recorded by Tori Rea, Molly Scott and Sarah Benson on the audio-cassette tape *We All Come From the Goddess* (Boston: Medicine Song Productions, 1986).

6) "Into The Silence" was inspired by Twylah Nitsch's description of the silence in *Indian Medicine Power, op.cit.*

7) *We All Come From the Goddess, op.cit.*

8) "The Goddess Is Alive" I first heard from Z. Budapest.

9) "Dear Friends" is an adaptation. The tune can be found with the "Kuan Yin" chant on *Reclaiming Chants, op.cit.*

10) "The Charge Of The Goddess" is an adaptation by Starhawk of the original by Doreen Valiente, quoted in Starhawk, *The Spiral Dance* (San Francisco: Harper & Row, 1979), pp. 76-77.

11) "By the Earth that is Her Body" is quoted by Starhawk in *The Spiral Dance*, 10th Anniversary Edition, (San Francisco: Harper and Row, 1989), p. 242.

Eclipse is an Earth-Witch/activist and mother. A visionary deeply involved in the empowerment of women and the return of the ancient religion of the Goddess, she leads workshops on ritual, Goddess religion, the Four Directions, astrology, tarot and healing. She is a co-founder of Earth Calls Network, an eco-feminist organization dedicated to challenging oppression and preserving the living body and spirit of the earth.

The recipient of six grants supporting her work, Eclipse has designed A.W.A.R.E. (Awareness With Art-Related Education), a program that brings ritual art, symbolism and expressive therapy together for children with behavioral and/or emotional disorders.

Eclipse hears the call of the Ancients as a call to honor the Earth and ourselves, a call to walk a path of beauty, power and courage. It is a call to dare to bring the political to the spiritual — to give birth to one's own visions.